THE HISTORY OF RUSSIA
FROM 1801 TO THE PRESENT

SOCIETIES AND CULTURES

RUSSIA

THE HISTORY
OF RUSSIA
FROM 1801 TO THE PRESENT

EDITED BY ROSINA BECKMAN

Britannica®
Educational Publishing

IN ASSOCIATION WITH

ROSEN
EDUCATIONAL SERVICES

Published in 2019 by Britannica Educational Publishing (a trademark of Encyclopædia Britannica, Inc.) in association with The Rosen Publishing Group, Inc.
29 East 21st Street, New York, NY 10010

Distributed exclusively by Rosen Publishing.
To see additional Britannica Educational Publishing titles, go to rosenpublishing.com.

First Edition

Britannica Educational Publishing
J.E. Luebering: Executive Director, Core Editorial
Andrea R. Field: Managing Editor, Compton's by Britannica

Rosen Publishing
Amelie von Zumbusch: Editor
Nelson Sá: Art Director
Brian Garvey: Series Designer/Book Layout
Cindy Reiman: Photography Manager
Bruce Donnola: Photo Researcher

Library of Congress Cataloging-in-Publication Data

Names: Beckman, Rosina, editor.
Title: The history of Russia from 1801 to the present / edited by Rosina Beckman.
Description: New York : Britannica Educational Publishing, in Association with Rosen Educational Services, 2019. | Series: Societies and cultures: Russia | Includes bibliographical references and index. | Audience: Grades 7–12.
Identifiers: LCCN 2017048983| ISBN 9781538303887 (library bound : alk. paper)
| ISBN 9781538303870 (pbk. : alk. paper)
Subjects: LCSH: Russia—History. | Soviet Union—History. | Russia (Federation)—History.
Classification: LCC DK40 .H576 2018 | DDC 947.01—dc23
LC record available at https://lccn.loc.gov/2017048983

Manufactured in the United States of America

Photo credits: Cover, p. 3 ID1974/Shutterstock.com; cover and interior pages (flag) fckncg/Shutterstock.com; cover and interior pages (emblem) N-sky/iStock/Thinkstock; p. 9 Keystone/Hulton Archive/Getty Images; p. 12 Heritage Images/Hulton Fine Art Collection/Getty Images; p. 15 Print Collector/Hulton Archive/Getty Images; p. 22 © Library of Congress, Washington, D.C., digital file number ppmsc 01514; p. 24 Culture Club/Hulton Archive/Getty Images; pp. 28-29 DEA/A. Dagli Orti/De Agostini/Getty Images; pp. 32, 43 Heritage Images/Hulton Archive/Getty Images; p. 36 Universal Images Group/Getty Images; pp. 47, 76 Bettmann/Getty Images; p. 51 © Encyclopaedia Britannica, Inc.; p. 53 ullstein bild/Getty Images; p. 57 Hulton Archive/Getty Images; p. 58 © Photo Harlingue/H. Roger-Viollet; p. 63 Universal History Archive/Universal Images Group/Getty Images; pp. 67, 73 © Photos.com/Thinkstock; p. 69 © Library of Congress, Washington, D.C.; p. 80 AFP/Getty Images; p. 84 Diana Walker/The LIFE Images Collection/Getty Images; p. 89 mark reinstein/Shutterstock.com; pp. 94-95, 99 Alexander Nemenov/AFP/Getty Images; pp. 102, 111 Sean Gallup/Getty Images; p. 105 Tatyana Makeyeva/AFP/Getty Images; p. 107 Vladimir Rodionov/AFP/Getty Images; p. 113 Anadolu Agency/Getty Images.

CONTENTS

During the 19th century, Russian tsars alternated between sometimes successful attempts at reform and returns to suppression, with Alexander I (ruled 1801–1825) and Alexander II (ruled 1855–1881) in the reformist camp and Nicholas I (ruled 1825–1855) and Alexander III (ruled 1881–1894) having a more autocratic outlook. Nicholas II, son of Alexander III, came to power in 1894. Weak-willed and indecisive, he was unsuited for the task of ruling a vast empire.

In 1914 Russia entered World War I. After three years of terrible losses, the Russian people rebelled against the tsar in March 1917. Nicholas II stepped down, and the country set up a temporary government. Nicholas and his family were later executed.

In November 1917 a faction of the revolutionaries called the Bolsheviks seized control of Russia. Led by Vladimir Lenin, the Bolsheviks set up a Communist government. The new government took Russia out of World War I.

Between 1918 and 1920 the Red Army successfully defended the new government against anticommunist forces in a civil war. The communist government officially established the Union of Soviet Socialist Republics on Dec. 30, 1922. The Russian Soviet Federated Socialist Republic dominated the Soviet Union for its entire 74-year history. It was by far the largest of the republics, and Moscow, its capital, was also the capital of the Soviet Union.

Following years of economic decline and political turmoil, the Soviet Union was dissolved in 1991. Boris

Yeltsin, leader of the former Russian republic, became president of the independent Russian Federation. Russia entered the post-Soviet era on the verge of economic collapse. Yeltsin's government began transforming the government-run Soviet economy into one based on private enterprise. However, privatization mainly benefited a handful of individuals whose political connections enabled them to buy companies for much less than they were worth. These "oligarchs" came to control huge segments of the Russian economy.

The Russian Revolution of 1917 took place in two stages. The February Revolution overthrew the imperial government, while the October Revolution placed the Bolsheviks in power. This protest in Petrograd (now St. Petersburg) happened during the second stage.

Vladimir Putin, Yeltsin's final prime minister, followed him as president. He declared his priorities to be reestablishing a strong state, restoring law and order, and relaunching economic reform. When the constitution prevented Putin from running for another term, Dmitry Medvedev, was elected president in 2008. In 2012, Putin was elected to a third term as president of Russia. His first months in office were marked by attempts to quash or marginalize protest movements against the government that had materialized in the past few years. Putin also took an active role in the events in neighboring Ukraine, resulting in Russia's annexation of Crimea in 2014.

CHAPTER ONE

THE REIGNS OF ALEXANDER I AND NICHOLAS I

When Alexander I came to the throne in March 1801, Russia was in a state of hostility with most of Europe, though its armies were not actually fighting. Its only ally was its traditional enemy, Turkey. The new emperor made peace with both France and Britain and restored normal relations with Austria. However his interest in internal reforms was frustrated by the reopening of war with Napoleon in 1805. Defeated at Austerlitz in December 1805, the Russian armies fought Napoleon in Poland in 1806 and 1807. Five years of peace followed the Treaty of Tilsit (1807), ended by Napoleon's invasion of Russia in 1812. After two years of heavy fighting, Russia won, emerging as Europe's greatest land power.

The mood was one of intense national pride: Orthodox Russia had defeated Napoleon, and therefore it was not only foolish but also impious to copy foreign models. Educated young Russians, however, felt otherwise. Masonic lodges and secret societies flourished in the early

Alexander I ruled Russia from 1801 to 1825. Although he alternately fought and befriended Napoleon I during the Napoleonic Wars, he ultimately helped form the coalition that defeated the French emperor.

1820s. From their deliberations emerged a conspiracy to overthrow the government. The conspirators, known as the Decembrists because they tried to act in December 1825 when the news of Alexander I's death became known and there was uncertainty about his successor, were defeated.

Nicholas I, who succeeded after his elder brother Constantine refused the throne, was deeply affected by these events and set himself against major political change. After the revolutions of 1848 in Europe, his opposition to all change, his suspicion of even mildly liberal ideas, and his insistence on an obscurantist censorship reached their climax. To the upper classes in central Europe, Nicholas I was the stern defender of monarchical legitimacy; to democrats around the world, he was "the gendarme of Europe" and the chief enemy of liberty. But the Crimean War (1853–56) showed that this giant had feet of clay. The vast empire was unable to mobilize, equip, and transport enough troops to defeat medium-size French and English forces under very mediocre command. Nicholas died in the bitter knowledge of general failure.

GOVERNMENT

The early years of Alexander's reign saw two periods of attempted reform. During the first, from 1801 to 1803, the tsar and four friends formed the so-called Unofficial Committee with the intention of drafting ambitious reforms. In the period from 1807 to 1812, he had as his chief adviser the liberal Mikhail Speransky. Both periods produced valuable administrative innovations, but neither produced real reform.

The discussions of the Unofficial Committee were part of an ongoing debate between enlightened oligarchy and enlightened autocracy. The proponents of oligarchy wished for the aristocracy to possess greater power. Their opponents, including the young count Pavel Stroganov, were against any limitation on the power of the tsar. Whereas the oligarchs wished to make the Senate an important centre of power and to have it elected by senior officials and country nobility, Stroganov maintained that this would leave the sovereign with "his arms tied." Alexander, however, never abandoned the idea of representative institutions. He encouraged Speransky to prepare in 1809 a draft constitution that included a pyramid of consultative elected bodies and a national assembly with some legislative powers. In 1819 he asked Nikolay Novosiltsev, a former member of the Unofficial Committee, to prepare a second, somewhat more conservative constitution. Neither was implemented, though Alexander used some features of the first, notably the institution of the State Council, out of their intended context.

In 1802 Alexander instituted eight government departments, or ministries. There was no question of a formal council of ministers, or of anything corresponding to a cabinet, and there was no prime minister. A committee of ministers coordinated the affairs of the departments, but its importance depended on circumstances and on individuals. When the tsar was abroad, the committee was in charge of internal affairs.

Under Nicholas I the committee of ministers continued to operate, but individual ministers were responsible only to the emperor. The centre of power to some extent shifted into the emperor's personal chancery. The Third Department of the chancery, created in 1826 under Count Aleksandr Benckendorff, was responsible for the security police. Its head was also chief of gendarmes, and the two offices were later united. The security force repressed all political activity that might be considered dangerous to the regime. The tsar considered the Third Department to be the defender of those unjustly treated

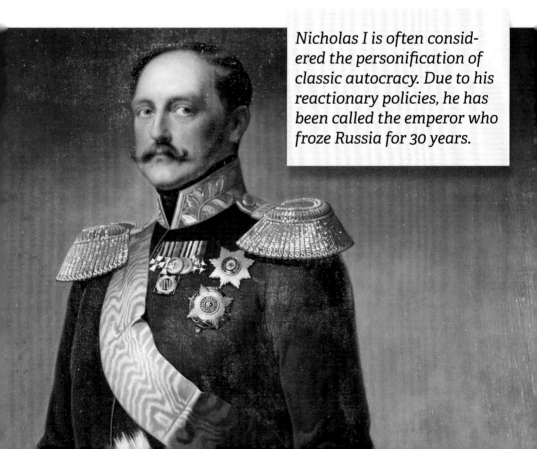

Nicholas I is often considered the personification of classic autocracy. Due to his reactionary policies, he has been called the emperor who froze Russia for 30 years.

by the powerful and rich. Some of the department's reports show officials who took these duties seriously, but as a whole it showed more talent for wasting time, repressing opposition, and stifling opinion than for redressing the grievances of the powerless.

Russia under Alexander I and Nicholas I was ruled by its bureaucracy. Russian bureaucrats were obsessed with rank and status. Rank was not so much a reward for efficient service as a privilege to be grasped and jealously guarded. In order to prevent able persons, especially of humble origin, from rising too quickly, great emphasis was placed on seniority. The size of the bureaucracy steadily increased, perhaps trebling in the first half of the century. It remained poorly paid. The government's poverty was caused by the underdeveloped state of the economy, by the fact that no taxes could be asked of the nobility, and by the cost of waging wars. Government officials were badly educated. They were reluctant to make decisions: responsibility was pushed higher and higher up the hierarchy, until thousands of minor matters ended on the emperor's desk. Since many small officials were unable to support their families, corruption existed on a mass scale. To a certain extent it was a redeeming feature of the regime: with less corruption the government would have been even slower, less efficient, and more oppressive.

SOCIAL CLASSES

No significant changes were made in the condition of the serfs in the first half of the century. Alexander I possessed a cautious desire for reform, but first war and then diplomacy diverted him. Nicholas disliked serfdom, but there were political hazards in eliminating it. The power of the central government extended down to the provincial governors and, more tenuously, down to the *ispravnik,* or chief official of the district, of which each province had several. The *ispravnik* was elected by the local nobility. Below the level of the district, the administration virtually ceased to operate: the sole authority was the serf owner. If serfdom were to be abolished, some other authority would have to take its place, and the existing bureaucratic apparatus was plainly inadequate. The Decembrist conspiracy in 1825 had greatly increased the tsar's distrust of the nobility. He was determined to avoid public discussion of reform, even within the upper class.

Only minor measures were taken to benefit the serfs on private estates. Opposition to serfdom grew steadily, not only among persons of European outlook but also among high officials. It seemed intolerable that in a great nation men and women could be owned. Serfdom was also obviously an obstacle to economic development.

Whether serfdom was contrary to the interests of serf owners is a more complex question. Certainly in parts of southern Russia where the soil was fertile, labour was plentiful, and potential profits in the grain trade with Europe were high, a landowner would do better if he could replace his serfs with paid agricultural labour and be rid of obligations to peasants whose labour he did not require. In other regions, where the population was

MINISTRY OF STATE DOMAINS

The one exception to the general bureaucratic stagnation during this period was the creation of the Ministry of State Domains, under General Pavel Kiselev. This became an embryonic ministry of agriculture, with authority over peasants who lived on state lands. These were a little less than half the rural population: in 1858 there were 19 million state peasants and 22.5 million private serfs. Kiselev set up a system of government administration down to the village level and provided for a measure of self-government under which the mayor of the *volost* (a district grouping several villages or peasant communes) was elected by male householders. There was also to be a *volost* court for judging disputes between peasants. Kiselev planned to improve medical services, build schools, establish warehouses for stocks of food in case of crop failure, and give instruction in methods of farming. Some progress was made, even if less than intended and often in a manner that provoked hostility or even violent riots; the personnel of the new ministry was no more competent than the bureaucracy as a whole.

scanty, serfdom provided the landowner with an assured labour supply. If it were abolished, he would have to pay more for his labour force or see it melt away. In large parts of northern Russia where the land was poor, many serfs made a living from crafts—in cottage industry or even in factories—and from their wages had to pay dues to their masters. The abolition of serfdom would deprive the serf owner of this income and leave him with only what he could make from farming.

Industry and trade made slow progress during these years. In the late 18th century, Russia had been, thanks to its Urals mines, one of the main producers of pig iron. In the next 50 years, it was eclipsed by Great Britain, Germany, and the United States. In cotton textiles and sugar refining, Russia was more successful. Count Egor Frantsevich Kankrin, minister of finance from 1823 to 1844, tried to encourage Russian industry by high protective tariffs. He set up schools and specialized institutes for the advancement of commerce, engineering, and forestry. Russia's exports of grain increased, though its share of total world trade remained about the same in 1850 as in 1800. The road system remained inadequate, but rail traffic between St. Petersburg and Moscow began in 1851.

The urban population grew significantly. There were a few prosperous merchants, well protected by the government. Some centres, such as Ivanovo in central Russia, with its textile industry, had the beginnings of an industrial working class. The rest of the inhabitants of the cities consisted of small tradesmen and artisans, together with serfs living in town with their owners' permission as household servants or casual labourers.

EDUCATION AND INTELLECTUAL LIFE

Alexander I's School Statute (1804) provided for a four-tier system of schools from the primary to the university level, intended to be open to persons of all classes. Several new universities were founded, and gymnasiums (pre-university schools) were established in most provincial capitals. Less was done at the lower levels, due to inadequate funds. In the latter part of Alexander's reign, education was supervised by Prince Aleksandr Nikolayevich Golitsyn. To combat what he believed to be dangerous irreligious doctrines emanating from western Europe, Golitsyn encouraged university students to spy on their professors and each other. Those who taught unacceptable ideas were dismissed or threatened with prison. Under Nicholas I there was some improvement. Count Sergey Uvarov, minister of education from 1833 to 1849, permitted a freer intellectual atmosphere, but he also began excluding children of the lower classes from the gymnasiums and universities, a policy continued under his successors.

Nevertheless, in increasing numbers the children of minor officials, small tradesmen, and especially priests were acquiring education. Together with the already Europeanized nobility, they formed a new cultural elite. Direct political criticism was prevented by the censorship of books and periodicals. Petty police interference made life disagreeable even for writers who were not much concerned with politics. Aleksandr Pushkin, Russia's greatest poet, got into trouble with the police for his opinions in 1824. After 1826 he lived an unhappy life in St. Petersburg, distrusted by the authorities and producing magnificent poetry until his death in a duel in 1837.

Censorship was not always efficient, and some censors were liberal. It became possible to express political ideas in the form of philosophical arguments and literary criticism. It was partly in intellectual periodicals and partly in discussions in the private houses of Moscow noblemen that the controversy between "Westernizers" and "Slavophiles" developed. It began with the publication of a "philosophical letter" by Pyotr Chaadayev in the periodical *Teleskop* in 1836.

The difference between Westernizers and Slavophiles was essentially that between radicals and conservatives. It set those who wished to pull the whole political structure down and replace it against those who preferred to knock down some parts and repair and refurnish others, bit by bit. Another basic difference was that the Slavophiles were Orthodox Christians and the Westernizers either atheists or, like the historian T.N. Granovsky, Deists. Westernizer Vissarion Belinsky described the Orthodox church in his famous "Letter to Gogol" (1847) as "the bulwark of the whip and the handmaid of despotism." He maintained that the Russian populace was "by its nature a profoundly atheistic people" and viewed the priesthood with contempt. These were but half-truths: the church was indeed subject to the government and upheld autocracy, and priests were often unpopular. Nevertheless the peasants and much of the upper and middle classes were devoted to the Orthodox faith.

The Slavophiles believed that Peter the Great had destroyed the once-happy partnership between tsar and

The eminent Russian literary critic Vissarion Belinsky is often called the father of the Russian radical intelligentsia. After being expelled from the University of Moscow in 1832, Belinsky earned his living as a journalist.

people when he imported foreign administrative models. They asked not for a legislative body of the Western type, but for a consultative assembly to advise the emperor. This was quite unacceptable to Nicholas, who saw himself as the political heir of Peter the Great. To the Westernizers, Peter was a symbol of radical change, not autocracy.

THE RUSSIAN EMPIRE

Russia in the 19th century was a multilingual, multireligious empire. Only about half the population was at the same time Russian by language and Orthodox by religion. The Orthodox were privileged in comparison with the other Christians; all Christians enjoyed a higher status than did the Muslims; and the latter were not so disadvantaged as were the Jews.

Nicholas expected all his subjects to obey him, but did not expect non-Russians to become Russians. The idea that Russians should have a status superior to that of other peoples of the empire was distasteful to Nicholas. Russian nationalism nevertheless received some support from Count Uvarov, who, in his famous report to the tsar in 1832, proclaimed three principles as "truly Russian": Orthodoxy, autocracy, and the national principle (*narodnost*). In 1833 Uvarov set up a new university in Kiev to spread Russian language and culture. Nicholas approved of this, for the Poles had been guilty of rebellion, but when the attempt was made to Russify the Germans of the Baltic provinces, he objected. The Baltic Germans were loyal subjects and provided admirable officers and officials; they were therefore allowed to preserve their culture and maintain their cultural and social domination over the Estonians and Latvians.

The most revolutionary of the Decembrist leaders, Pavel Pestel, had insisted that all non-Russian peoples of the empire except the Poles "completely fuse their nationality with the nationality of the dominant people." Another group of Decembrists, however, the Society of United Slavs, believed in a federation of free Slav peoples, including some living under Austrian and Turkish rule. In 1845 this idea was put forward in a different form in the Brotherhood of SS. Cyril and Methodius, in Kiev. This group believed that a federation of Slav peoples should include the Ukrainians, whom they claimed were not a part of the Russian nation but a distinct nationality. The

The celebrated Ukrainian poet Taras Shevchenko was a member of the Brotherhood of SS. Cyril and Methodius. Nothing did more to crystallize Ukrainian as a literary language than Shevchenko's poetry.

society was crushed by the police, but Ukrainian national consciousness, though still confined to an educated minority, was growing.

During the first half of the century, Russia made substantial conquests in Asia. In the Caucasus the kingdom of Georgia united voluntarily with Russia in 1801, and other small Georgian principalities were conquered in the next years. Persia ceded northern Azerbaijan, including the peninsula of Baku, in 1813 and the Armenian province of Erivan (Yerevan) in 1828. The mountain peoples of the northern Caucasus, however, proved more redoubtable. The Chechens, led by Shāmil, resisted Russian expeditions from 1834 until 1859, and the Circassians were not finally crushed until 1864. In the 1840s Russian rule was established over the pastoral peoples of Kazakhstan. In East Asia, Russian ships explored the lower course of the Amur River and discovered the straits between Sakhalin and mainland Asia in 1849. The Russian-American Company, founded in 1799, controlled parts of coastal Alaska.

FOREIGN POLICY

At the beginning of the 19th century, Russian foreign policy concentrated on the neighbouring countries with which it had been preoccupied since the 16th century: Sweden, Poland, and Turkey. The policy toward these countries determined Russian relations with France, Austria, and Great Britain.

Russo-Swedish relations were settled during the Napoleonic era. When Napoleon met with Alexander at Tilsit, he gave the latter a free hand to proceed against Sweden. After two years of war, the Swedish government ceded Finland to the tsar in 1809. Alexander became grand duke of Finland, but Finland was not incorporated into the Russian Empire, and its institutions were fully respected. When Napoleon's former marshal, Jean-Baptiste Bernadotte, was elected heir to the Swedish throne in 1810, he showed no hostility toward Russia. In 1812 Bernadotte recognized the tsar's position in Finland in return for Russian support for his plan to annex Norway from Denmark. Thereafter relations between Russia and Sweden were not seriously troubled.

Alexander I, influenced by his Polish friend Prince Adam Czartoryski, had plans for the liberation and unity of Poland, which had ceased to exist as a state when it was partitioned among Russia, Prussia, and Austria in the 18th century. After his defeat by Napoleon in 1805, Alexander abandoned those plans in favour of an alliance with Prussia. In 1807 Napoleon established a dependency called the Grand Duchy of Warsaw and in 1809 increased its territory at the expense of Austria. Alexander's attempts to win the Poles to his side in 1811 and persuade Austria to make concessions to them failed. When Napoleon invaded Russia in 1812, he had 100,000 first-class Polish troops fighting for him. After Napoleon's defeat, Alexander protected the Poles against the demands of Russian nationalists who wanted revenge and sought to create a Polish kingdom comprising the territories annexed by Russia and Prussia in the 18th century. He was opposed at the Congress of Vienna in 1814–15 by Austria and Britain. The ensuing kingdom of Poland, though nominally autonomous, was to be in permanent union with the Russian Empire and consisted of only part of the Prussian and Russian conquests.

Alexander was popular in Poland for a time. But competing claims for the borderlands, which had belonged to the former grand duchy of Lithuania, made real reconciliation between Poles and Russians impossible. Russians argued that most of Lithuania had been part of "the Russian land" until the 14th century, and the Poles that it had been Polish since the 16th. Alexander had some sympathy for the Polish point of view, but political forces in Russia strongly opposed it. The disappointment of Polish hopes for Lithuania led to growing tension between Warsaw and

St. Petersburg in the late 1820s, culminating in a revolt in November 1830 and war the following year. This ended in the defeat of the Poles and the exile of thousands of political leaders and soldiers to western Europe.

Turkey had long been the object of Russian territorial expansion. The policy was reinforced by religious motives—a romantic desire to liberate Constantinople (Istanbul), the holy city of Orthodoxy—but more important in the 19th century was the desire to export Russian grain through the Black Sea. Russia sought to dominate Turkey as a powerful ally. When this policy was successful, Russia supported the Ottoman Empire and made no territorial demands. When it failed, Russia sought to undermine Turkey by supporting rebellious Balkan peoples or by war.

In the periods of hostility, the main object of Russian expansion was the area later known as Romania—the Danubian principalities of Moldavia and Walachia. In 1812 Moldavia was partitioned between Russia and Turkey: the eastern half was annexed to Russia. Russian armies marched through the principalities in the war of 1828–29 and occupied them until 1834. In 1848 the Russians returned, with Turkish approval, to suppress the revolution that had broken out in Bucharest. It seemed only a matter of time before Russia annexed the Romanian principalities. Russia's defeat in the Crimean War, however, prevented this.

The Crimean War (1853–56) pitted Russia against Great Britain, France, and Turkey. It was fought in Crimea

The November Insurrection of 1830–31 unsuccessfully tried to overthrow Russian rule in the Kingdom of Poland, as well as in the Polish provinces of western Russia and parts of Lithuania, Belorussia (now Belarus), and Ukraine.

due to Austrian diplomacy. In June 1854 the Russian government accepted the Austrian demand that Russian troops withdraw from the Danubian principalities, and in August Austrian troops entered. It is arguable whether the presence of Austrian troops benefited Russia by preventing French and British forces from marching on Ukraine or damaged Russia by preventing its troops from marching on Istanbul. The tsar resented the Austrian action as showing ingratitude toward the power that had saved Austria from Hungarian rebels in 1849. Unable to attack in the principalities, the British and French sent an expedition to Crimea to destroy the Russian naval base at Sevastopol. It was there that the war dragged out its course. The war showed the inefficiency of Russia's top military command and of its system of transport and supply. The Russian armies nevertheless won victories over the Turks in the Caucasus, and the defense of Sevastopol for nearly a year was a brilliant achievement.

CHAPTER TWO

FROM ALEXANDER II TO NICHOLAS II

Defeat in Crimea made Russia's lack of modernization clear, and the first step toward modernization was the abolition of serfdom. The new tsar, Alexander II (reigned 1855–81), believed that the dangers to public order of dismantling the existing system, which had deterred Nicholas I from action, were less than the dangers of leaving things as they were.

EMANCIPATION AND REFORM

The Ministry of the Interior spearheaded the reform efforts. The bulk of the landowning class was determined, if it could not prevent abolition of serfdom, to give the freed peasants as little as possible. The settlement, proclaimed on February 19, 1861, was a compromise. (The date in the New Style—or Gregorian calendar, which was adopted in the 1580s by Catholic Europe, but was not used in Russia until 1918—is March 3). Peasants were freed from servile status, and a procedure was laid down by which they could become landowners. The government paid the landowners compensation and recovered the cost in annual "redemption payments" from the peasants. The terms were generally unfavourable to the peasants.

The main beneficiary of the reform was arguably not the peasant but the state. A new apparatus of government was established to replace the authority of the serf owner. From the *ispravnik*, who in 1862 ceased to be elected by the nobility and became an appointed official of the Ministry of the Interior, the official hierarchy now stretched down to the village notary, who was assisted by an elder elected by an assembly of householders. The lowest effective centre of power was the village commune (*obshchina*), an institution of great antiquity with the power to redistribute land for the use of its members and determine the crop cycle, that now also became responsible for collecting taxes on behalf of the government.

Further reforms followed emancipation. A system of elected assemblies at the provincial and county levels was introduced in 1864. These assemblies, called zemstvos, were elected by all classes including the peasants, although the landowning nobility had a disproportionately large share of both the votes and the seats. The zemstvos could levy taxes to fund schools, public health, roads, and other social services. In 1864 a major judicial reform was completed. Russia received a system of law courts based on European models, with irremovable judges and courts of appeal. Justices of the peace, elected by the county zemstvos, were instituted for minor offenses. An organized, modern legal

Alexander II's liberal education and distress at the outcome of the Crimean War inspired him toward a great program of domestic reforms, the most important being the emancipation of the serfs in 1861.

profession arose and soon achieved high standards. The old system of endless delays and judicial corruption rapidly disappeared. There were, however, gaps in the system. Regardless of the courts, the Ministry of the Interior had the power to banish persons whom it regarded as politically dangerous.

REVOLUTIONARY ACTIVITIES

During the 1860s revolutionary groups began to appear. The outstanding figure was the socialist writer N.G. Chernyshevsky. In 1861–62 revolutionary leaflets were distributed in St. Petersburg, ranging from the demand for a constituent assembly to a passionate appeal for insurrection. An unsuccessful attempt on the tsar's life in 1866 led Alexander to pick extremely conservative advisers. Nevertheless, some worthwhile reforms happened. In 1870 the main cities of Russia were given elected municipal government (on a very narrow franchise), and in 1874 a series of military reforms was completed by the establishment of universal military service.

In the 1870s revolutionary activity revived. Its centre was the university youth, influenced by socialist ideas derived from Europe but adapted to Russian conditions. These young people saw in the peasantry the potential for revolutionary action. In 1873–74 hundreds of the youth, including women, "went to the people," invading the countryside and seeking to rouse the peasants with their speeches. The peasants did not understand, and the police arrested the young revolutionaries. Some were sentenced to prison, and hundreds deported to remote provinces or to Siberia. It became clear that no progress could be expected from overt action: conspiratorial action was the only hope. In 1876 a new party was founded that took the title of Zemlya i Volya ("Land and Freedom"). Some of its members favoured assassination of prominent officials in reprisal for the maltreatment of their comrades and to pressure the government for Western-type political liberties. Experience also had shown them that, while the peasants were too scattered to be an effective force and were in any case too apathetic, workers in the cities offered a more promising audience. This faction was opposed by others in the party who deprecated assassination, continued to pay more attention to peasants than workers, and were indifferent to the attainment of political liberties. In 1879 the party split. The violent wing took the name Narodnaya Volya ("People's Will") and made its aim the assassination of Alexander II. After several unsuccessful attempts, the tsar was fatally wounded by a bomb on March 1 (March 13, New Style), 1881. The main leaders of the group were caught by the police, and five were hanged.

Before his death the tsar had been considering reforms that would have introduced a few elected representatives into the apparatus of government. His successor, Alexander III (reigned 1881–94), instead reaffirmed the principle of autocracy. In 1882 Alexander appointed Dmitry Tolstoy minister of the interior. Konstantin Pobedonostsev (Alexander's former tutor and the procurator of the

Holy Synod) and Tolstoy crafted the reactionary policies that followed. Education was further restricted, the work of the zemstvos hampered, and village communes were brought under closer control in 1889 by the institution of the "land commandant" (*zemsky nachalnik*)—an official appointed by the Ministry of the Interior who interfered in all aspects of peasant affairs. The office of elected justice of the peace was abolished, and the government was authorized to assume emergency powers when public order was said to be in danger. By this time Russian public officials had become better paid and educated and less corrupt, but they retained their arrogant contempt for the public and especially for the poorer classes.

The economic development of the following decades created new social tensions and brought into existence new social groups, from whom active opposition once more developed. The zemstvos were in growing conflict with the central authorities. Even their efforts at non-political social improvement met with obstruction. The Ministry of the Interior, once the centre of Russia's best reformers, became a stronghold of resistance. In the obscurantist view of its leading officials, only the central government had the right to care for the public welfare, and zemstvo initiatives were undesirable usurpations of power. Better that nothing should be done at all than that it should be done through the wrong channels. This attitude was manifested in 1891, when crop failures led to widespread famine; government obstruction of relief efforts was widely—though often unfairly—blamed for

Alexander III was an opponent of representative government and an ardent supporter of Russian nationalism. He supported the Russification of national minorities and the persecution of non-Orthodox religious groups.

the peasantry's sufferings. The revival of political activity may be dated from this year. It was accelerated by the death of Alexander III in 1894 and the succession of his son Nicholas II (reigned 1894–1917), who antagonized the zemstvo liberals by publicly describing their aspirations for reforms as "senseless dreams." In the late 1890s moderate liberalism was common among elected zemstvo members, who were largely members of the landowning class and hoped to establish a consultative national assembly. A more radical attitude, combining elements of liberalism and socialism, was found in the professional classes of the cities. The growth of an industrial working class provided a mass basis for socialist movements, and by the end of the century interest in politics even began to penetrate the peasantry.

ECONOMIC AND SOCIAL DEVELOPMENT

Though many peasants improved their position after emancipation, agriculture remained underdeveloped and widespread poverty persisted. This was partly due to the government's indifference to agriculture. Economic policy was motivated by the desire for national and military power. This required the growth of industry, and great efforts were made to encourage it. Agriculture was regarded mainly as a source of revenue to pay for industry and the armed forces. Taxes paid by peasants filled the state's coffers. The redemption payments drained the peasants' resources, though a gradual fall in the value of money reduced that burden in time. Consumption taxes, especially on sugar, tobacco, matches, and oil, affected the peasants, and so did import duties. In 1894 the government introduced a liquor monopoly that drew enormous revenues from the peasants. The techniques and tools of agriculture remained primitive and farm output low; virtually nothing was done to instruct peasants in modern methods.

Another cause of peasant poverty was overpopulation. The vast landmass of Russia was sparsely populated, but the number of persons employed in agriculture per unit of arable land, and relative to output, was extremely high. There was a vast and increasing surplus of labour in Russian villages. Peasants competed with each other to lease land from the landlords' estates, driving rents up. The existence of the large estates came to be resented more and more and prompted demands for further land redistribution.

Capitalist development did occur, if rather slowly. A rapid growth of railways came in the 1870s, and in the same decade the exploitation of petroleum began at Baku in Azerbaijan. Only in the 1890s did the demand for iron and steel, created by the railway program and the military, begin to be satisfied on a large scale within Russia. By the end of the century there was a massive metallurgical industry in Ukraine, based on the iron ore of Krivoy Rog and the coal of the Donets Basin. Poland was another metallurgical centre. The iron industry of the Urals, which lost much of its labour force when the serfs became free to leave, lagged far behind. Textiles were concentrated in the central provinces of Moscow and Vladimir; by the end of the century they were drawing much of their raw cotton from the newly conquered lands of Central Asia. Baku was booming, especially as a supplier of petroleum to the Moscow region. St. Petersburg had begun to develop important engineering and electrical industries. Count Sergey Witte, minister of finance from 1892 to 1903, put Russia on the gold standard in 1897 and encouraged foreign investors.

Industrial growth produced an urban working class. Workers were unskilled, badly paid, overworked, and miserably housed. This was especially true of central Russia, where the labour surplus kept wages low. In St. Petersburg, where it was harder to recruit workers, the transformation of the urban poor into a modern working class made the most progress. St. Petersburg employers were also less hostile to government legislation on behalf of the workers.

In 1882 Finance Minister Nikolay Khristyanovich Bunge introduced an inspectorate of labour conditions and limited hours of work for children. In 1897 Witte introduced a maximum working day of 11.5 hours for all workers, male or female, and of 10 hours for those engaged in night work. Trade unions were not permitted, though several attempts were made to organize them illegally. The Ministry of the Interior, being more interested in public order than in businessmen's profits, occasionally showed concern for the workers. Strikes were forbidden but occurred anyway.

THE COMMUNE

Another economic problem was the inefficiency of the peasant commune, which had the power to redistribute holdings according to the needs of families and dictate the rotation of crops. This hampered enterprising farmers and protected incompetent ones. Nevertheless the commune ensured a living for everyone and stood for values of solidarity and cooperation. Russian officials also found it useful as a means of collecting taxes and keeping the peasants in order. The 1861 settlement did provide a procedure by which peasants could leave the commune, but it was complicated and little used. The communal system predominated in northern and central Russia, and individual peasant ownership was widespread in Ukraine and in the Polish borderlands. In 1898 about 198 million acres (80 million hectares) of land were under communal tenure in European Russia, while about 54 million (22 million) were under individual tenure.

The value of the commune was disputed. The Ministry of the Interior, which stood for paternalism and public security at all costs, favoured the commune in the belief that it was a bulwark of conservatism, traditional values, and loyalty to the tsar. The Socialist Revolutionaries saw it as, at least potentially, the natural unit of a future socialist republic. The Ministry of Finance, concerned with developing capitalism, objected to the commune as an obstacle to economic progress; it envisioned a prosperous minority of individual farmers as a basis of a more modern type of Russian conservatism. The Social Democrats agreed that the commune must be replaced by capitalist ownership, but saw this only as the next step toward a socialist revolution led by urban workers.

Russia's industrial progress differed from classical Western capitalism in that the motivation of Russian industrial growth was political and military, and the driving force was government policy. Russian and foreign capitalists provided the resources and the organizing skill, and they were richly rewarded. The richness of their rewards accounted for a second difference from classical capitalism: Russian capitalists were completely satisfied with the political system as it was. Whereas English and French capitalists had material and ideological reasons to fight against absolute monarchs and aristocratic upper classes, Russian businessmen accepted autocracy.

EDUCATION AND IDEAS

In the last half of the 19th century, the word "intelligentsia" came into use in Russia. Essentially, the intelligentsia consisted of persons with a modern education and a passionate preoccupation with general political and social ideas. Its nucleus was to be found in the professions of law, medicine, teaching, and engineering, which grew in numbers and social prestige as the economy became more complex. Yet it also included private landowners, bureaucrats, and even army officers. The intelligentsia was opposed to the existing political and social system, which coloured its attitude toward culture in general. In particular, works of literature were judged according to whether they furthered the cause of social progress.

Professional revolutionaries were largely recruited from the intelligentsia. The lack of civil liberties and the prohibition of political parties made it necessary for socialists to use conspiratorial methods. Illegal parties had rigid centralized discipline. Yet the emergence of the professional revolutionary, imagined in romantically diabolical terms in the *Revolutionary Catechism* of Mikhail Bakunin and Sergey Nechayev in 1869 and sketched more realistically in *What Is to Be Done?* by Vladimir Ilyich Ulyanov, better known as Lenin, in 1902, was not entirely due to the circumstances of the underground political struggle. The revolutionaries were formed also by their sense of mission, by their absolute conviction that they knew best the interests of the masses.

Russian revolutionary socialism at the end of the century was divided into two main streams, each subdivided into a section that favoured conspiratorial tactics and one that aimed at a mass movement. The Socialist Revolutionary Party (Socialist Revolutionaries; founded in 1901 from a number of groups more or less derived from Narodnaya Volya) at first hoped that Russia could bypass capitalism; they later aimed to limit its operation and build a socialist order based on village communes. The land was to be socialized but worked by peasants on the principle of "labour ownership." The Russian Social-Democratic Workers' Party (Social Democrats; founded in 1898 from a number of illegal working-class groups) believed that the future lay with industrialization and a socialist order based on the working class. The Socialist Revolutionaries were divided between their extreme terrorist wing, the "Fighting Organization," and a broader and looser membership that at one end merged imperceptibly with radical middle-class liberalism. The Social Democrats were divided between Lenin's group, which took the name "Bolshevik," and a number of other groups that were by no means united but that came to be collectively known as "Menshevik." Among the issues dividing these groups were Lenin's preference for rigid discipline, the Mensheviks' attempts to create a mass labour movement of the western European type and greater willingness to cooperate with nonsocialist liberals, and Lenin's greater estimation of peasants as a potential revolutionary force.

Mikhail Bakunin was the chief propagator of 19th-century anarchism, a prominent Russian revolutionary agitator, and a prolific political writer.

RUSSIFICATION POLICIES

After the Crimean War, the Russian government attempted to introduce a pro-Russian program in Poland. This proved unacceptable to the Poles, and in January 1863 armed rebellion broke out. This rebellion was put down, being suppressed with special severity in the Lithuanian and Ukrainian borderlands. To punish the Polish gentry for their part in the insurrection, Russian authorities carried out a land reform on terms exceptionally favourable to the Polish peasants. The reform was followed by an anti-Polish policy in education and other areas. By the 1880s the language of instruction even in primary schools in areas of purely Polish population was Russian. At first, the Poles acquiesced in their defeat, but in the 1890s two strong, if illegal, anti-Russian political parties appeared—the National Democrats and the Polish Socialist Party.

After 1863 the authorities also severely repressed all signs of Ukrainian nationalist activity. In 1876 all publications in Ukrainian, other than historical documents, were prohibited. In Eastern Galicia, however, which lay just across the Austrian border and had a population of several million Ukrainians, not only the language but also political activity flourished. There the great Ukrainian historian Mikhail Hrushevsky and the socialist writer Mikhail Drahomanov published their works; Ukrainian political literature was smuggled across the border. In the 1890s small illegal groups of Ukrainian democrats and socialists existed on Russian soil.

From the 1860s the government embarked on a policy designed to strengthen the position of the Russian language and nationality in the borderlands of the empire. This policy is often described as "Russification." Though Russian was to be the lingua franca, the government never explicitly demanded that its non-Russian subjects abandon their own languages, nationalities, or religions. Still, conversions to Orthodoxy were welcomed, and converts were not allowed to revert to their former religions. The government policy of Russification found its parallel in the overtly Russian nationalist tone of several influential newspapers and journals. For most supporters of Russification, however, the policy's main aim was to consolidate a Russian national identity and loyalty at the empire's centre and to combat the potential threat of imperial disintegration in the face of minority nationalism.

By the late 19th and early 20th century, some of the most prominent objects of Russification were peoples who had shown consistent loyalty to the empire and now found themselves confronted by government policies that aimed to curtail their rights and privileges. The Germans of the Baltic provinces were deprived of their university, and their secondary schools were Russified. The attempt to abolish many aspects of Finnish autonomy united the Finns in opposition to St. Petersburg in the 1890s. In 1904 the son of a Finnish senator assassinated the Russian governor-general, and passive resistance to Russian policies was almost universal. Effective passive resistance also occurred among the traditionally Russophile Armenians of the Caucasus when the Russian authorities began to interfere with the organization of the Armenian church and close the schools maintained from its funds.

Of the Muslim peoples of the empire, those who suffered most from Russification were the Tatars of the Volga valley. Attempts by the Orthodox church to convert Muslims and the rivalry between Muslims and Orthodox to convert small groups practicing traditional religions caused growing mutual hostility. By the end of the century the Tatars had developed a substantial merchant class. Modern schools were creating a new Tatar educated elite that was increasingly receptive to modern democratic ideas. In Central Asia, on the other hand, modern influences had barely made themselves felt, and there was no Russification. In those newly conquered lands, Russian colonial administration was paternalistic and limited: like the methods of "indirect rule" in the British and French empires, it made no systematic attempt to change old ways.

The position of the Jews was hardest of all. Due to their history and religious traditions, as well as of centuries of social and economic discrimination, the Jews were overwhelmingly concentrated in commercial and intellectual professions. They were thus prominent both as businessmen and as political radicals, hateful to the bureaucrats as socialists and to the lower classes as capitalists. The pogroms, or anti-Jewish riots, which broke out in various localities in the months after the assassination of Alexander II, effectively ended any dreams for assimilation for Russia's Jewish community. At this time there also arose the oft-repeated accusation that anti-Semitic excesses were planned and staged by the authorities, not only in Ukraine in 1881 but also in Kishinev in 1903 and throughout the Jewish Pale of Settlement in 1905. The view of government-sponsored pogroms has not, however, been corroborated by documental evidence. Indeed, the officials in St. Petersburg were too concerned with maintaining order to organize pogroms that might pose a direct threat to that order. However, local government officials were certainly at least remiss in their duties in protecting Jewish lives and properties and even in cahoots with the anti-Semitic rioters. The 1881 pogrom wave resulted in the promulgation in May 1882 of the notorious "temporary rules," which further restricted Jewish rights and remained in effect to the very end of the Russian Empire.

This engraving shows Jews being expelled from St. Petersburg. While the city was not within the Jewish Pale of Settlement—the area in which Jews were permitted to live—veterans and more educated Jews were at times permitted to live there

FOREIGN POLICY

During the second half of the 19th century, Russian foreign policy gave about equal emphasis to the Balkans and East Asia. The friendship with Germany and Austria weakened, and in the 1890s the Triple Alliance of Germany, Austria-Hungary, and Italy opposed a Dual Alliance in France and Russia.

In 1876 the Serbo-Turkish War produced an outburst of Pan-Slav feeling in Russia. Under its influence, but also in pursuit of traditional strategic aims, Russia declared war on Turkey in April 1877. After overpowering Turkish resistance at the fortress of Pleven in Bulgaria, the Russian forces advanced almost to Istanbul. By the Treaty of San Stefano of March 1878 the Turks accepted the creation of a large independent Bulgarian state. Fearing that this would be a Russian vassal, Britain and Austria-Hungary opposed the treaty. At the international Congress of Berlin, held in June 1878, Russia had to accept a much smaller Bulgaria. The Russian people regarded this as a bitter humiliation. In the 1890s, despite the pro-Russian sentiment of many Serbs and Bulgarians, neither country's government was much subject to Russian influence. Russian policy on the whole tended to support the Turkish government. In 1897 an Austro-Russian agreement was made on spheres of influence in the Balkans.

The Russian government, alarmed by indications of a closer cooperation between the Triple Alliance and Britain, reluctantly turned toward France. The French needed an ally against both Germany and Britain; the Russians needed French capital, in the form both of loans to the Russian government and of investment in Russian industry. The Franco-Russian alliance was signed in August 1891 and was supplemented by a military convention.

Russia established diplomatic and commercial relations with Japan by three treaties between 1855 and 1858. In 1860, by the Treaty of Beijing, Russia acquired from China a long strip of Pacific coastline south of the mouth of the Amur. The Russians began to build the naval base of Vladivostok. In 1867 the Russian government sold Alaska to the United States for $7.2 million. The Treaty of St. Petersburg between Russia and Japan in 1875 gave Russia sole control over all of Sakhalin and gave Japan the Kuril Islands.

The Russian conquest of Turkistan, south of the Kazakh steppes, began in the 1860s. This was watched with distrust by the British authorities in India, and fear of Russian interference in Afghanistan led to the Anglo-Afghan War of 1878–80. In the 1880s Russian expansion extended to the Turkmen lands on the east coast of the Caspian Sea, whose people offered stiffer military resistance. The Russian conquest of Merv in 1884 caused alarm in Kolkata (Calcutta), and in March 1885 a clash between Russian and Afghan troops produced a major diplomatic crisis between Britain and Russia. An agreement on frontier delimitation was reached in September 1885, and for the next decades Central Asian affairs had little effect on Anglo-Russian relations.

In 1894–95 the long-standing rivalry between the Japanese and Chinese in Korea led to a war between the two empires, which the Japanese won. Russia faced the choice of collaborating with Japan (with which relations had recently been fairly good) or allying with China. The tsar chose the second policy, largely under the influence of Count Witte. Together with the French and German governments, the Russians demanded that the Japanese return to China the Liaodong Peninsula. Russia concluded an alliance with China in 1896, which included the establishment of the Chinese Eastern Railway, linking Siberia with Vladivostok and owned and operated by Russia. In 1898 the Russian government went further and acquired the Liaodong Peninsula from China. There the Russians built a naval base in ice-free waters at Port Arthur (Lüshun; now in Dalian, China). They also obtained extraterritorial rights of ownership and management of a southern Manchurian railroad that was to stretch from north to south, linking Port Arthur with the Chinese Eastern Railway at the junction of Harbin. When in 1900 the European powers sent armed forces to relieve their diplomatic missions in Beijing, besieged by the Boxer Rebellion, the Russian government took the opportunity to bring substantial military units into Manchuria. All of this bitterly antagonized the Japanese. They might have been willing, nonetheless, to write off Manchuria as a Russian sphere of influence provided that Russia recognize Japanese priority in Korea, but the Russian government would not do this. The British government, fearing that

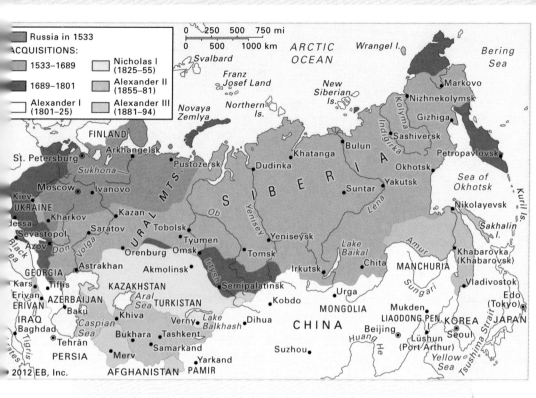

This map traces Russia's expansion between 1533 and 1894. The last of the many additions to the empire's territory were all in Asia.

Russia would interfere with the interests of Britain in other parts of China, made an alliance with Japan in January 1902. On the night of January 26/27 (February 8/9, New Style), 1904, Japanese forces made a surprise attack on Russian warships in Port Arthur, and the Russo-Japanese War began.

CHAPTER THREE

THE LAST YEARS OF TSARDOM

The Russo-Japanese War brought a series of Russian defeats on land and sea, culminating in the destruction of the Baltic fleet in the Tsushima Strait. The defeat finally brought to a head a variety of political discontents simmering back at home. First the professional strata, especially in the zemstvos and municipalities, organized a banquet campaign in favour of a popularly elected legislative assembly. Then, on January 9 (January 22, New Style), 1905, the St. Petersburg workers, led by Georgy Gapon (of the Assembly of Russian Factory Workers), marched on the Winter Palace to present Emperor Nicholas with a petition containing even wider-ranging demands. They were met by troops who opened fire on them, killing about 130.

THE REVOLUTION OF 1905–06

News of this massacre spread quickly. Soon the whole empire was in uproar. There were student demonstrations, workers' strikes, peasant insurrections, and mutinies in both the army and navy. The peasants organized themselves through their traditional village assembly, the *mir*, to decide how to seize the land or property of the landlords. The workers, on the other hand, created the Soviet of Workers' Deputies. These new institutions, consisting of elected delegates from the factories and workshops of a whole town, organized the strike movement, negotiated with the employers and police, and sometimes kept up basic municipal services during the crisis.

The revolutionary movement reached its climax in October 1905, with the declaration of a general strike and the formation of a soviet (council) in St. Petersburg itself.

Protests during the Russian Revolution of 1905 ranged from liberal rhetoric to strikes and included student riots and terrorist assassinations. This painting shows a barricade in the streets of Moscow during the uprising.

Most cities, including the capital, were paralyzed. Witte recommended that the government yield to the demands of the liberals and create an elected legislative assembly. The tsar reluctantly consented, in the manifesto of October 17 (October 30, New Style), 1905. It did not end the unrest, however. In several towns, armed bands of monarchists, known as Black Hundreds, organized pogroms against Jewish quarters and attacked students and left-wing activists. In Moscow the soviet unleashed an armed insurrection in December, which had to be put down with artillery, resulting in considerable loss of life. Peasant unrest and mutinies in the armed services continued well into 1906 and even 1907.

Throughout the period from 1905 to 1907, disorders were especially violent in non-Russian regions of the empire, where the revolutionary movement took on an ethnic dimension. A campaign of terrorism, waged by the Maximalists of the Socialist Revolutionary Party against policemen and officials, claimed hundreds of lives in 1905–07. The police felt able to combat it only by infiltrating their agents into the revolutionary parties and particularly into the terrorist detachments of these parties. This use of double agents (or agents provocateurs, as they were often known) did much to demoralize both the revolutionaries and the police and to undermine the reputation of both with the public at large. The nadir was reached in 1908, when it was disclosed that Yevno Azef, longtime head of the terrorist wing of the Socialist Revolutionary Party, was also an employee of the department of police.

The split in the Social Democratic Party was deepened by the failure of the 1905 revolution. Both Mensheviks and Bolsheviks agreed that a further revolution would be needed but disagreed fundamentally on how to bring it about. The Mensheviks favoured cooperation with the bourgeois parties in the Duma, the new legislative assembly, in order to legislate civil rights and then use them to organize the workers for the next stage of the class struggle. The Bolsheviks regarded the Duma purely as a propaganda forum, and Lenin drew from 1905 the lesson that in Russia, where the bourgeoisie was weak, the revolutionaries could combine the bourgeois and proletarian stages of the revolution by organizing the peasantry as allies of the workers. In 1912 the split with the Mensheviks was finalized when the Bolsheviks called their own congress in Prague that year, claiming to speak for the entire Social Democratic Party.

THE STATE DUMA

The October Manifesto had split the opposition. The professional strata, now reorganizing themselves in liberal parties, accepted it and set about trying to make the new legislature, the State Duma, work in the interest of reform. The two principal socialist parties, the Socialist Revolutionaries and the Social Democrats, saw the manifesto as just a first step and the Duma (which at first they boycotted) as merely a tool to project their revolutionary ideas.

Alongside the Duma there was to be an upper chamber, the State Council, half of its members appointed by the emperor and half elected by established institutions such as the zemstvos and municipalities, business organizations, the Academy of Sciences, and so on. Both chambers had budgetary rights, the right to veto any law, and the ability to initiate legislation. Nevertheless the government would be appointed, as before, by the emperor, who had the right to dissolve the legislative chambers at any time or pass emergency decrees when they were not in session.

The first elections, held in spring 1906, produced a relative majority for the Constitutional Democratic Party (Kadets), a group drawn largely from the professional strata that wished for a full constitutional monarchy and to grant autonomy to the non-Russian nationalities. The next largest caucus, the Labour Group (Trudoviki), included many peasants and some socialists who had ignored their comrades' boycott. The two parties demanded amnesty for political prisoners, equal rights for Jews, autonomy for Poland, and the expropriation of landed estates for the peasants. These demands were totally unacceptable to the government, which used its powers to dissolve the Duma.

In early 1907 new elections were held. The Social Democrats, having abandoned their boycott, came in as the third largest party, behind the Kadets and the Trudoviki. Premier Pyotr Arkadyevich Stolypin advised the tsar to once again dissolve the Duma.

Some of Nicholas's advisers wished to abolish the Duma altogether. Instead, he and Stolypin altered the electoral law in favour of landowners, wealthier townsfolk, and Russians to the detriment of peasants, workers, and non-Russians. The Third Duma, elected in autumn 1907, and the Fourth, elected in autumn 1912, were therefore more congenial to the government. The leading caucus in both Dumas was the Union of October 17 (known as the Octobrists), whose strength was among the landowners of the Russian heartland.

The conservative statesman Pyotr Stolypin initiated far-reaching agrarian reforms to improve the legal and economic status of the peasantry, general economy, and political stability of imperial Russia.

Although the legislative achievements of the Duma were meagre, it should not be written off as an ineffective body. It voted credits for a planned expansion of education that was on target to introduce compulsory primary schooling by 1922. Although it could not create or bring down governments, it exerted real pressure on ministers, especially during the budget debates in which even foreign and military affairs

The Siberian peasant and mystic Rasputin's treatment of Alexis, the hemophiliac heir to the Russian throne, made him an influential favourite at the court of Nicholas II and Alexandra.

(constitutionally the preserve of the emperor alone) came under the deputies' scrutiny. These debates were extensively reported in the newspapers and enormously intensified public awareness of political issues.

The workers' movement revived in 1912, after a disorder at the Lena gold mines, where some 200 workers were killed by troops. Strikes and demonstrations broke out in many cities, culminating in the erection of barricades in St. Petersburg in July 1914. This time, the workers were on their own: there was no sign that peasants, students, or professional people were prepared to join their struggle.

One area where the failure to reform had serious effects was in the church. Most prelates and clergymen wanted to see the Orthodox church given greater independence, perhaps by restoring the patriarchate and assigning authority within the church to a synod elected by clergy and laity. Many also favoured internal reform by strengthening the parish, ending the split between parish and monastic clergy, and bringing liturgy and scriptures closer to the people. Instead the church remained under secular domination and fell increasingly under the influence of Grigory Yefimovich Rasputin, a *starets* (holy

AGRARIAN REFORMS

The 1905 revolution showed that the village commune was not a guarantor of stability, but rather a promoter of unrest. Stolypin aimed to undermine it as part of his program for restoring order. He also aimed to give peasant households the chance to leave the commune and to consolidate their strip holdings, enclosing them as privately owned smallholdings.

The reforms enjoyed some success. By 1915 some 20 percent of communal households had left the communes, and about 10 percent had taken the further step of consolidating their strips into one holding. All over the country, land settlement commissions were surveying, redrawing boundaries, and negotiating with the village assemblies on behalf of the new smallholders. Not unnaturally, individual withdrawals often aroused resentment, and reform worked more effectively when whole villages agreed to consolidate and enclose their strips. Many households, both within and outside the commune, joined cooperatives to purchase seeds and equipment or to market their produce. Some peasants from the more densely settled regions of Russia migrated to the open spaces of Siberia and northern Turkistan, attracted by free land, subsidies for travel, and specialist advice.

man) of dubious reputation who became a favourite of the imperial couple.

WORLD WAR I AND THE FALL OF THE MONARCHY

Excluded as a serious player in East Asia, Russia focused on the Balkans, where the vulnerability of the Habsburg monarchy and the Ottoman Empire were generating an increasingly volatile situation. Besides, the Octobrists and many of the Rights who supported the government in the Duma took a great interest in the fate of the Slav nations of the region and favoured more active Russian support for them.

Negotiations between the Russian foreign minister, Aleksandr Petrovich Izvolsky and his Austrian counterpart, Alois, Count Lexa von Aehrenthal did not go in Russia's favor. Austria occupied Bosnia and Herzegovina unilaterally, without making Russia any reciprocal concessions. Russia protested but was unable to achieve anything, as Germany threw its support behind Austria. The public humiliation forced Izvolsky to resign, and his successor, Sergey Dmitriyevich Sazonov, set about building an anti-Austrian bloc of Balkan states, including Turkey. This failed, but instead Russia was able to sponsor a Serbian-Greek-Bulgarian-Montenegrin alliance, which was successful in the First Balkan War against Turkey (1912–13). This seemed to herald a period of greater influence for Russia in the Balkans. Austria, however, demanded that the recently enlarged Serbia be denied an outlet to the Adriatic Sea by the creation of a new state of Albania. Russia supported the Serbian desire for an Adriatic port, but the European powers decided in favour of Austria. The Balkan alliance then fell apart, with Serbia and Greece fighting on the side of Turkey in the Second Balkan War (1913).

The assassination of Archduke Franz Ferdinand in June 1914 placed Russia in a difficult situation. If Russia let Serbia down and yielded to Austrian pressure, it would cease to be taken seriously as a participant in Balkan affairs and its prestige as a European great power would be seriously compromised. The alternative was to escalate the Balkan conflict to the point where Germany would come in behind Austria and a wider war would ensue. Russia chose the second alternative. Nicholas II hoped that, by mobilizing only those forces on his border with Austria-Hungary, he could avoid both German intervention and escalation into world war. Instead, the result was World War I.

In 1914 the Franco-Russian alliance proved its value. The German army could have crushed either France or Russia but not both. The Russian invasion of East Prussia in August 1914 failed, but it caused the Germans to withdraw troops from their western front and left the French to win the First Battle of the Marne (September 6–12, 1914). Turkey's entry into the war on the German side was a major setback, since it not only created a new front in the Caucasus (where the Russian armies performed rather well) but, by closing the straits, enormously reduced the supplies that the Allies could deliver to Russia. When the Central Powers launched a spring offensive in 1915, the Russian army was already short of munitions. The Germans and Austrians occupied Poland and began advancing into the western provinces and the Baltic region, unleashing a flood of refugees.

After the military reverses of 1915, the Duma and State Council pressed the government to become more responsive to public opinion. The centre and left of the State Council combined with all the centre parties in the Duma to form a Progressive Bloc. Its aim was a "government enjoying public confidence," whose ministers would be drawn partly from the legislative chambers. The bloc called for a broad program of political reform, including freeing political prisoners, repealing discrimination against religious minorities, emancipating the Jews, autonomy for Poland, the elimination of the remaining legal disabilities suffered by peasants, the repeal of anti-trade-union legislation, and the democratization of local government. Premier Ivan Logginovich Goremykin rejected the plan as an attempt to undermine the autocracy.

For Nicholas, only the autocratic monarchy could sustain effective government and avoid social revolution and the disintegration of the multinational empire. In August 1915 Nicholas announced that he was taking personal command of the army, leaving the empress in charge of the government. He decamped to Mogilyov, in Belarusia, but played only a ceremonial role, allowing his military chief of staff, General Mikhail Vasilyevich Alekseyev, to act as true commander in chief. During the next few months Nicholas dismissed all eight ministers who had supported the Progressive Bloc. He insisted on maintaining ultimate power and prevented capable ministers from coordinating the administration of the government and war effort. From afar he ordained frequent pointless ministerial changes, partly under the influence of his wife and Rasputin. Even loyal monarchists despaired of the situation,

Nicholas II visits a munitions factory in St. Petersburg in 1914. A lack of munitions would prove one of the major problems for Russia in the early years of World War I.

and in December 1916 Rasputin was murdered in a conspiracy involving some of them.

In the end it was the economic effect of the war that proved too much for the government. The munitions shortage prompted a partly successful reorganization of industry to concentrate on military production, and by late 1916 the army was better supplied than ever. But life on the home front was grim. The German and Turkish blockade choked off most imports. The food supply was affected by the call-up of numerous peasants and by the diversion of transport to other needs. The strain of financing the war generated accelerating inflation, with which the pay of ordinary workers failed to keep pace. Strikes began in the summer of 1915 and increased during the following year, culminating in a huge strike centred on the Putilov armament and locomotive works in Petrograd (the name given to St. Petersburg in 1914) in January 1917.

The February (March, New Style) Revolution began among the food queues of the capital, which started calling for an end to autocracy. Soon workers from most of the major factories joined the demonstrations. The vital turning point came when Cossacks summoned to disperse the crowds refused to obey orders and troops in the city garrison mutinied and joined insurgents. The workers and soldiers rushed to re-create the institution they remembered from 1905, the Soviet of Workers' and Soldiers' Deputies. Other towns and army units throughout the empire followed their example. Faced with the threat of a civil war, the military high command abandoned Nicholas II in the hope that the Duma leaders would contain the revolution and provide effective leadership of the domestic front.

By agreement between the Petrograd soviet and the Duma, a Provisional Government formed, headed by Prince Georgy Yevgenyevich Lvov and consisting mainly of Kadets and Octobrists. On March 2 (March 15, New Style), this government's emissaries reached Pskov, where the emperor had become stranded in his train, attempting to reach Petrograd. He abdicated, bringing to an end the Romanov dynasty.

CHAPTER FOUR

SOVIET RUSSIA

The February Revolution of 1917 was spontaneous, leaderless, and fueled by deep resentment over the economic and social conditions that had prevailed in imperial Russia under Tsar Nicholas. The country, having been sucked into World War I, found the strains of fighting a modern war with a premodern political and economic system intolerable. The tsar fell short as a war leader and was unable to cope with the burdens of being head of state. Hardly a hand was raised in support when the imperial order collapsed in February (March, New Style) 1917. The key factor had been the defection of the military. Without this instrument of coercion, the tsar could not survive. Most Russians rejoiced, but a political vacuum had been created.

The Provisional Government (established to govern until elections for a Constituent Assembly could be held) was undone by war, economic collapse, and its own incompetence. It postponed hard decisions—what to do about land seizures by the peasants, for example—for the Constituent Assembly. A fatal mistake was its continued prosecution of the war. Disgruntled peasant-soldiers wanted to quit the army. They did not perceive Germany to be a threat to Russian sovereignty, and they deserted in droves to claim their piece of the landlord's estate. Industrial decline and rising inflation radicalized workers and cost the Provisional Government the support of the professional middle classes. The Bolshevik slogan of "All power to the soviets" was attractive. The government seemingly spoke for the country, but in reality it represented only the middle class; the soviets represented the workers and peasants. Moderate socialists—Mensheviks and Socialist Revolutionaries—dominated the Petrograd and Moscow soviets after February, but the radical Bolsheviks began to win local elections and by September had a majority in the Petrograd Soviet.

THE OCTOBER (NOVEMBER) REVOLUTION

A turning point in the struggle for power was the attempt by General Lavr Kornilov, who had been appointed commander in chief, to take control of Petrograd in August 1917 and wipe out the soviet. Prime Minister Aleksandr Kerensky, who had been negotiating with Kornilov, turned around and labeled him a traitor, perceiving his attack as an attempt to overthrow the government. Kerensky agreed to the arming of the Petrograd soviet, but after the failed coup the weapons were retained. The Bolsheviks could now consider staging an armed uprising.

The October Revolution began when Kerensky, angered by claims that the Bolsheviks controlled the Petrograd garrison, sent troops to close down two Bolshevik newspapers. The Bolsheviks, led by Leon Trotsky, feared that Kerensky would attempt to disrupt the Second All-Russian Congress, scheduled to open in October. They reacted by sending troops to take over key communications and transportation points in the city. Lenin emerged from hiding to urge the Bolsheviks to press forward and overthrow the Provisional Government, which they did on the morning of October 26. After the almost bloodless siege, Lenin proclaimed that power had passed to the soviets.

Lenin speaks to a cheering crowd during the Russian Revolution. Few individuals in modern history had as profound an effect on their times or evoked as much heated debate as Lenin.

At the Second All-Russian Congress of Soviets in October (November, New Style) 1917, Lenin secured a solely Bolshevik government—the Council of People's Commissars, or Sovnarkom. The Bolsheviks also had a majority in the Soviet Central Executive Committee, which was accepted as the supreme law-giving body. It was, however, the Central Committee of the Communist Party, the Bolsheviks' party, in which true power came to reside. This governmental structure was to last until the convocation of the Constituent Assembly in January 1918. However, Lenin disbanded the assembly when it became clear that the Bolsheviks did not hold a majority, setting the stage for civil war. In the immediate post-October days, a majority of the Bolshevik Central Committee favoured a coalition government, and Lenin eventually had to give in. Some Socialist Revolutionaries were added in December 1917, but the coalition government remained in office only until March 1918, when the Bolsheviks accepted the defeatist Treaty of Brest-Litovsk, ending Russian participation in World War I. The Socialist Revolutionaries, disagreeing with the terms of the treaty, resigned. The Bolsheviks had the Congress of Soviets under control by the summer of 1918. Local soviets continued to defy the Bolsheviks but to no avail.

THE CIVIL WAR

By this point, only part of Russia—Moscow, Petrograd, and much of the industrial heartland—was under Bolshevik control. Ukraine slipped under German influence, and the Mensheviks held sway in the Caucasus. The country-side belonged to the Socialist Revolutionaries. Given the Bolshevik desire to dominate the former empire, civil war was inevitable.

The Red Army was formed in February 1918, and Leon Trotsky became its leader. He was to reveal great leadership and military skill, fashioning a rabble into a formidable fighting force. The Reds were opposed by the "Whites," anticommunists led by former imperial officers. There were also the "Greens" and the anarchists, who fought the Reds and were strongest in Ukraine; their most talented leader was Nestor Makhno. The Allies (Britain, the United States, Italy, and a host of other states)

The Red Army was recruited exclusively from among workers and peasants and immediately faced the problem of creating a competent officers' corps. Trotsky met this problem by mobilizing former officers of the imperial army.

intervened on the White side and provided much matériel and finance. By mid-1920 the Reds had consolidated their hold on the country.

The feat of winning the Civil War and the organizational methods adopted to do so made a deep impact on Bolshevik thinking. The Bolsheviks were ruthless in their pursuit of victory. The Cheka (a forerunner of the notorious KGB), or political police, was formed in December 1917 to protect communist power. By the end of the Civil War it had become a powerful force. Among the targets of the Cheka were Russian nationalists who objected strongly to the bolshevization of Russia. They regarded bolshevism as alien and based on western European and not Russian norms. Lenin was always mindful of "Great Russian" chauvinism, which was one reason he never permitted the formation of a separate Russian Communist Party apart from that of the Soviet Union. Russia, alone of the U.S.S.R.'s 15 republics, did not initially have its own communist party.

NEW ECONOMIC POLICY

Soviet Russia adopted its first constitution in July 1918 and fashioned treaties with other republics such as Ukraine. The latter was vital for Russia's economic viability, and Bolshevik will was imposed. It was also imposed in the Caucasus, where Georgia, Armenia, and Azerbaijan were tied to Bolshevik Russia by 1921. Russia lost control of the Baltic states and Finland, however. Lenin's nationality policy assumed that nations would choose to stay in

WAR COMMUNISM

Lenin did not favour moving toward a socialist economy after October, because the Bolsheviks lacked the necessary economic skills. He preferred state capitalism, with capitalist managers staying in place but supervised by the workforce. The Civil War caused the Bolsheviks to adopt a more severe economic policy known as War Communism, characterized chiefly by the expropriation of private business and industry and the forced requisition of grain and other food products from the peasants. The Bolsheviks subsequently clashed with the labour force, which understood socialism as industrial self-management. Ever-present hunger exacerbated the poor labour relations, and strikes became endemic, especially in Petrograd. The Bolsheviks pressed ahead, using coercion as necessary. The story was the same in the countryside. Food had to be requisitioned in order to feed the cities and the Red Army. The Reds informed the peasants that it was in their best interests to supply food, because if the landlords came back the peasants would lose everything.

a close relationship with Russia, but this proved not to be the case. Many wanted to be independent in order to develop their own brand of national communism. The comrade who imposed Russian dominance was Joseph Stalin. As commissar for nationalities, he sought to ensure that Moscow rule prevailed.

Forced requisitioning led to peasant revolts, and the Tambov province revolt of 1920 in particular forced

Lenin to change his War Communism policy. The Bolshevik leadership were willing to slaughter the mutinous sailors of the Kronstadt naval base in March 1921, but they could not survive if the countryside turned against them. They would simply starve to death. A tactical retreat from enforced socialism was deemed necessary. Key sectors of the economy—heavy industry, communications, and transport—remained in state hands, but light and consumer-goods industries were open to the entrepreneur. The economy was back to its 1913 level by the mid-1920s, which permitted a debate on the future. All Communist Party members agreed that the goal was socialism, and this meant the dominance of the industrial economy. The working class, the natural constituency of the Communist Party, had to grow rapidly.

Soviet Russia gave way to the Union of Soviet Socialist Republics (U.S.S.R.) in 1922, but this did not mean that Russia gave up its hegemony within the new state. As before, Moscow was the capital, and it dominated the union. Lenin's death in January 1924 set off a succession struggle that lasted until the end of the decade. Joseph Stalin eventually outwitted Trotsky, Lenin's natural successor, and other contenders.

THE STALIN ERA

Stalin, a Georgian, surprisingly turned to "Great Russian" nationalism to strengthen the Soviet regime. During the 1930s and '40s he held the Russians up as the elder brother for non-Slavs to emulate.

Industrialization developed first and foremost in Russia (followed by Ukraine) and expanded rapidly under Stalin. The industrialization of the Caucasus and Central Asia began during the 1930s, and it was the Russians, aided by the Ukrainians, who ran the factories. The labour force was also predominantly Russian, as was the emerging technical intelligentsia. Collectivization, though, met with resistance in rural areas. Ukraine in particular suffered harshly at Stalin's hands because of forced collectivization. He encountered strenuous resistance there, for which he never forgave the Ukrainians. His policies thereafter brought widespread starvation to that republic, especially in 1932–33, when millions died.

Stalin's nationality policy initially promoted native cultures, but this changed in the

One of the most ruthless dictators of modern times was Joseph Stalin, the despot who transformed the Soviet Union into a major world power. The victims of his campaigns of political terror included some of his followers.

late 1920s. Stalin appears to have perceived that the non-Russians were becoming dangerously self-confident and self-assertive. He came to the conclusion that a Sovietized Russian elite would be a more effective instrument of modernization. In the non-Russian republics, Russians and Ukrainians were normally second secretaries of the Communist Party and occupied key posts in the government and political police. Diplomats were predominantly Russian. The Soviet constitution of 1936 was democratic—but only on paper. It rearranged the political and nationality map. The boundaries of many autonomous republics and oblasts were fashioned so as to prevent non-Russians from forming a critical mass. Moscow's fear was that they would circumvent central authority. For example, Tatars found themselves in the Tatar (Tatarstan) and Bashkir (Bashkiriya) autonomous republics, although Tatars and Bashkirs spoke essentially the same language. Tatars also inhabited the region south of Bashkiriya and northern Kazakhstan, but this was not acknowledged, and no autonomous republic was established. Moscow played off the various nationalities to its own advantage. This policy was to have disastrous long-term consequences for Russians, because they were seen as imperialists bent on Russifying the locals. New industry usually attracted Russian and Ukrainian labour rather than the locals, and this changed the region's demographic pattern.

Victory over Germany in World War II precipitated an upsurge of Russian national pride. Russia, in the guise of the U.S.S.R., had become a great power. War reparations went first and foremost to Russian factories. When the United Nations was first set up, in 1945, Stalin did not insist that Russia have a separate seat like the Ukrainian and Belorussian republics had, which suggests he regarded the U.S.S.R.'s seat as Russia's. The advent of the Cold War in the 1940s led to Stalin tightening his grip on his sphere of influence in eastern and southeastern Europe. Russian was imposed as the main foreign language, and Russian economic experience was copied. A dense network of treaties enmeshed the region in the Russian web.

The Bolsheviks had always been suspicious of minorities on their frontiers, and the first deportation of non-Russian minorities to Siberia and Central Asia began in the 1920s. Russian Cossacks were removed forcibly from their home areas in the north Caucasus and elsewhere because of their opposition to collectivization and communist rule. On security grounds, Stalin deported entire small nationality groups, such as the Chechen and Ingush, from 1944 onward. They were accused of collaborating with the Germans. The Volga Germans were deported in the autumn of 1941 lest they side with the advancing Wehrmacht. Altogether, more than 50 nationalities, embracing about 3.5 million people, were deported to various parts of the U.S.S.R. The vast majority of these were removed from European Russia to Asiatic Russia.

The late Stalin period witnessed campaigns against Jews and non-Russians. Writers and artists who dared to claim that Russian writers and cultural figures of the past had learned from the West were pilloried. Russian chauvinism took over, and anything that was worth inventing was claimed to have been invented by a Russian.

THE KHRUSHCHEV ERA

Nikita Khrushchev won the power struggle for leadership that ensued after Stalin's death in 1953. Khrushchev's landmark decisions in foreign policy and domestic programs changed the direction of the Soviet Union, bringing détente with the West and a relaxation of rigid controls within the country. A Russian who had grown up in Ukraine, Khrushchev rose as an agricultural specialist under Stalin. He took it for granted that Russians

Correspondents from Western nations described Khrushchev as a man of enormous energy and drive, talkative, sociable, earthy, tough, and shrewd. With great self-confidence he took colossal gambles in both foreign and domestic policy.

had a natural right to instruct less-fortunate nationals. This was especially evident in the non-Slavic republics of the U.S.S.R. and in eastern and southeastern Europe. His nationality policies reversed the repressive policies of Stalin. This allowed many peoples to return to their homelands within Russia, the Volga Germans and the Crimean Tatars being notable exceptions.

As head of the party Secretariat (which ran the day-to-day affairs of the party machine) after Stalin's death, Khrushchev used that vehicle to promote his campaigns. *Pravda* ("Truth"), the party newspaper, served as his mouthpiece. His main opponent in the quest for power, Georgy M. Malenkov, was skilled in administration and headed the government. *Izvestiya* ("News of the Councils of Working People's Deputies of the U.S.S.R."), the government's newspaper, was Malenkov's main media outlet. Khrushchev's agricultural policy involved a bold plan to rapidly expand the sown area of grain. He chose to implement this policy on virgin land in the north Caucasus and west Siberia, lying in both Russia and northern Kazakhstan. The Kazakh party leadership was not enamoured of the idea, however, not wanting more Russians in their republic. The result was that Kazakh leadership was dismissed, and the new first secretary was a Malenkov appointee; he was soon replaced by Leonid I. Brezhnev, a Khrushchev protégé who eventually replaced Khrushchev as the Soviet leader. Thousands of young communists descended on Kazakhstan to grow crops where none had been grown before.

Khrushchev's so-called "secret speech" at the 20th Party Congress in 1956 had far-reaching effects on both foreign and domestic policies. Through its denunciation of Stalin, it substantially destroyed the infallibility of the party. The congress softened the party's hard-line foreign policy. De-Stalinization had unexpected consequences, especially in eastern and southeastern Europe in 1956, where unrest became widespread. The Hungarian uprising in that year was brutally suppressed, which stoked anti-Russian fires.

Successes in space exploration under Khrushchev's regime brought great applause for Russia. He improved relations with the West, establishing a policy of peaceful coexistence that eventually led to the signing of the Nuclear Test-Ban Treaty of 1963. But he was eccentric and blunt, traits that sometimes negated his own diplomacy. Khrushchev's offhanded remarks occasionally caused massive unrest in the world. He told the United States, "We will bury you," and boasted that his rockets could hit a fly over the United States, which convinced the Americans to increase their defense budget. This accelerated the arms race with the United States, when his objective had been the opposite. His plan to install nuclear weapons in Cuba for local Soviet commanders to use should they perceive that the Americans were attacking brought the world seemingly close to the brink of nuclear war.

Khrushchev genuinely wanted to improve the lot of all Soviet citizens. Under his leadership there was a cultural thaw. Russian writers who had been suppressed began to publish again. Western ideas about democracy penetrated universities and academies. These were to leave their mark on a whole generation of Russians.

THE BREZHNEV ERA

After Khrushchev came the triumvirate of Leonid I. Brezhnev, Aleksey N. Kosygin, and N.V. Podgorny. The first was the party leader, the second headed the government, and the third became chairman of the Presidium of the Supreme Soviet, a ceremonial position. By the late 1960s Brezhnev was clearly the dominant leader. He ensured an unprecedented stability of cadres within the Communist Party and the bureaucracy, allowing for the spread of corruption in the Soviet political and administrative structures. However, it was also under Brezhnev that the U.S.S.R. acquired nuclear parity with the United States and was recognized as a world superpower. Détente flourished in the 1970s but was disrupted by the Soviet invasion of Afghanistan in December 1979.

Under Brezhnev, Russia dominated the U.S.S.R. as never before. Three-fourths of the defense industries were in Russia, and the republic accounted for about three-fourths of the Soviet gross national product. The rapid expansion of the chemical, oil, and gas industries boosted exports so that Russia earned most of the union's hard-currency income. The middle class grew in size, as did its average salary, which more than doubled in two decades. Ownership of consumer goods, such as refrigerators and cars, became a realistic expectation for a growing part

Brezhnev gave the Soviet Union a formidable military-industrial base capable of supplying large numbers of the most modern weapons, but in so doing he impoverished the rest of the Soviet economy.

of the population. The availability of medical care, good housing, and higher education reached unprecedented levels. But the income from the sale of Russia's natural resources also allowed the Soviet regime to evade undertaking necessary but potentially politically dangerous structural economic reforms.

Kosygin recognized the seriousness of the problems facing the Soviet economic structure and attempted to implement reforms in 1965 and 1968, but the Brezhnev leadership stopped them. By the mid-1970s, growth in the non-natural resource sector of the economy had slowed greatly. The Soviet economy suffered from a lack of technological advances, poor-quality products unsatisfactory to both Soviet and foreign consumers, low worker productivity, and highly inefficient factories. The government was spending an increasing amount of its money trying to feed the country. Soviet agriculture suffered from myriad problems, the resolution of which required radical reforms. In sum, by the 1970s, continued economic stagnation posed a serious threat to the world standing of the U.S.S.R. and to the regime's legitimacy at home.

The state gradually lost its monopoly on information control. A counterculture influenced by Western pop music spread rapidly, aided by the rise of the audio-cassette. The widespread teaching of foreign languages further facilitated access to outside ideas. By the end of the Brezhnev era, the Russian intelligentsia had rejected Communist Party values. The party's way of dealing with uncomfortable critics, such as the dissenting novelist Aleksandr Solzhenitsyn, was to deport them. These exiles then became the voice of Russian culture abroad. The academician Andrey Sakharov could not be imprisoned, for fear of Western scientists cutting off contact with the Soviet Union, but he was exiled to the closed city of Gorky (now Nizhny Novgorod). Sakharov was released in 1986 and returned to Moscow. In 1989 he was elected to the Congress of People's Deputies, and many of the causes for which he originally suffered became official policy under Mikhail Gorbachev's reforms.

THE GORBACHEV ERA

When Brezhnev died in 1982, most elite groups understood that the Soviet economy was in trouble. Due to senility, Brezhnev had not been in effective control of the country during his last few years, and Kosygin had died in 1980. The Politburo was dominated by old men, and they were overwhelmingly Russian. Non-Russian representation at the top of the party and the government had declined over time. Yury V. Andropov and then Konstantin Chernenko led the country from 1982 until 1985, but their administrations failed to address critical problems. Andropov mistakenly believed that the economic stagnation could be remedied by greater worker discipline and cracking down on corruption.

When Gorbachev became head of the Communist Party in 1985, he launched *perestroika* ("restructuring"). His team was more heavily Russian than that of his predecessors. It seems that initially even Gorbachev believed that only minor reforms were needed. He aimed to increase economic growth while increasing capital investment to improve the technological basis of the Soviet economy. His goal was quite plain: to bring the Soviet Union up to par economically with the West. After two years, Gorbachev concluded that deeper structural changes were necessary. In 1987–88 he pushed through reforms that went less than halfway to the creation of a semi-free market system. The consequences of this semi-mixed economy brought economic chaos to the country and great unpopularity to Gorbachev.

Gorbachev launched *glasnost* ("openness") as the second vital plank of his reform efforts. He believed that the opening up of the political system—essentially, democratizing it—was the only way to overcome inertia in the political and bureaucratic apparatus. In addition, he believed that economic and social recovery required the inclusion of people in the political process. *Glasnost* allowed the media more freedom of expression, and editorials complaining of depressed conditions and of the government's inability to correct them began to appear.

As the economic and political situation began to deteriorate, Gorbachev concentrated his energies on increasing his authority. He became a constitutional dictator—but only on paper. His policies were simply not put into practice. When he took office, Yegor Ligachev was made head of the party's Central Committee Secretariat, one of the two main centres of power (with the Politburo) in the Soviet Union. Ligachev made it difficult for Gorbachev to use the party apparatus to implement his views on *perestroika*.

By the summer of 1988, however, Gorbachev was able to take the party out of the day-to-day running of the economy. This responsibility would pass to the local soviets. A new parliament, the Congress of People's Deputies, was convened in the spring of 1989, with Gorbachev presiding. The new body superseded the Supreme Soviet as the highest organ of state power. It elected a new Supreme Soviet, and Gorbachev, who had opted for an executive presidency modeled on the U.S. and French systems, became the Soviet president, with broad powers. This meant that all the republics, including first and foremost Russia, could have a similar type of presidency. Moreover, Gorbachev radically changed Soviet political life when he removed the constitutional article that had made the Communist Party of the Soviet Union the only legal political organization.

Gorbachev understood that the defense burden, perhaps equivalent to 25 percent of the gross national product, was crippling the country. It had led to cuts in expenditures in education, social services, and medical care, which hurt the regime's domestic legitimacy. Gorbachev therefore transformed Soviet foreign policy. He traveled abroad extensively and was brilliantly successful in convincing foreigners that the U.S.S.R. was no longer an international threat. His changes in foreign policy led to the democratization of eastern Europe and the end of the Cold War. On the other hand, Gorbachev's policies

After summits in 1985, 1986, and 1987, Gorbachev and U.S. President Ronald Reagan signed the Intermediate-Range Nuclear Forces (INF) Treaty on December 8, 1987, in Washington, D.C.

deprived the Soviet Union of ideological enemies, which in turn weakened the hold of Soviet ideology over the people.

As the U.S.S.R.'s economic problems became more serious (e.g., rationing was introduced for some basic food products for the first time since Stalin) and calls for faster political reforms and decentralization began to increase, the nationality problem became acute for Gorbachev. Limited force was used in Georgia, Azerbaijan, and the Baltic states to quell problems, though Gorbachev was never prepared to use systematic force in order to reestablish the centre's control. The reemergence of Russian nationalism seriously weakened Gorbachev as the leader of the Soviet empire.

In 1985 Gorbachev brought Boris Yeltsin to Moscow to run that city's party machine. Yeltsin was a deputy from Moscow to the Congress of People's Deputies in 1989. When the Congress of People's Deputies elected the Supreme Soviet as a standing parliament, Yeltsin was not chosen. However, a Siberian deputy stepped down in his favour. Yeltsin for the first time had a national platform. In parliament he pilloried Gorbachev, the Communist Party, corruption, and the slow pace of economic reform. Despite the bitter opposition of Gorbachev, Yeltsin was elected president of the Russian parliament.

When Gorbachev launched an all-union referendum about the future Soviet federation in March 1991, Russia and several other republics added supplementary questions. One of the Russian questions was whether the voters supported a directly elected president. They were, and they chose Yeltsin. He used his newfound legitimacy to promote Russian sovereignty, to advocate and adopt radical economic reform, to demand Gorbachev's resignation, and to negotiate treaties with the Baltic republics, in which he acknowledged their right to independence. Soviet attempts to discourage Baltic independence led to a bloody confrontation in Vilnius in January 1991, after which Yeltsin called upon Russian troops to disobey orders that would have them shoot unarmed civilians.

Yeltsin's politics reflected the rise of Russian nationalism. Russians began to view the Soviet system as working for its own political and economic interests at Russia's expense. There were complaints that the "Soviets" had destroyed the Russian environment and had impoverished Russia in order to maintain their empire and subsidize the poorer republics. Yeltsin and his supporters demanded Russian control over Russia and its resources. In June 1990 the Russian republic declared sovereignty, establishing the primacy of Russian law within the republic. This effectively undermined all attempts by Gorbachev to establish a Union of Sovereign Socialist Republics. Yeltsin had appeared willing to go along with this vision but, in reality, wanted Russia to dominate the new union and replace the formal leading role of the Soviet Union. The Russian parliament passed radical reforms that would introduce a market economy, and Yeltsin cut funding to many Soviet agencies based on Russian soil. Clearly, he wished to rid Russia of the encumbrance of the Soviet Union.

CHAPTER FIVE

POST-SOVIET RUSSIA

A poorly executed coup attempt occurred August 19–21, 1991, bringing an end to the Communist Party and accelerating the movement to disband the Soviet Union. It was carried out by hard-line Communist Party, KGB, and military officials attempting to avert a new liberalized union treaty and return to the old-line party values. The most significant anti-coup role was played by Yeltsin, who brilliantly grasped the opportunity to promote himself and Russia. He demanded the reinstatement of Gorbachev as U.S.S.R. president, but, when Gorbachev returned from house arrest in Crimea, Yeltsin set out to demonstrate that he was the stronger leader. Yeltsin banned the Communist Party in Russia and seized all of its property.

THE YELTSIN ERA

The U.S.S.R. legally ceased to exist on December 31, 1991. The new state, called the Russian Federation, set off on the road to democracy and a market economy without any clear conception of how to complete such a transformation. Like most of the other former Soviet republics, it entered independence in a state of serious disorder and economic chaos.

ECONOMIC REFORMS

Upon independence, Russia faced economic collapse. The new Russian government not only had to deal with the economic problems from the Gorbachev period, but also needed to transform the entire Russian economy. In 1991 alone, gross domestic product (GDP) dropped by about one-sixth, and the budget deficit was approximately one-fourth of GDP. Price controls on most goods led to scarcity. By 1991 few items essential for everyday life were available in traditional retail outlets. The entire system of goods distribution was on the verge of disintegration.

The transformation of the command economy to a market-based one was fraught with difficulties and had no historical precedent. Since the central command economy had existed in Russia for more than 70 years, the transition to a market economy proved more difficult for Russia than for the countries of eastern Europe. Russian reformists had no clear plan, and circumstances did not give them time to put together a reform package. In addition, the reformists had to balance the necessities of economic reform with powerful vested interests.

In an effort to bring goods into stores, the Yeltsin government removed price controls on most items in

January 1992—the first essential step toward creating a market-based economy. However, it also spurred inflation, which became a daily concern for Russians, whose salaries and purchasing power declined as prices for even the most basic goods continued to rise. The government frequently found itself printing money to fill holes in the budget and to prevent failing factories from going bankrupt.

During the Soviet era the factory had often been the base of social services, providing benefits such as childcare, vacations, and housing. If industries collapsed,

In 1991 Boris Yeltsin became the first popularly elected leader in Russia's history, guiding the country through a stormy decade of political and economic retrenching until his resignation on the eve of 2000.

the government would have had to make provisions not only for unemployed workers but also for a whole array of social services. The government's infrastructure could not cope with such a large additional responsibility. Yet the inflation caused by keeping these factories afloat led to waning support for both Yeltsin and economic reform, as many average Russians struggled to survive. Starved for cash, factories reverted to paying workers and paying off debts to other factories in kind. It was not uncommon for workers to go months without being paid and to get paid in, for example, rubber gloves or crockery, either because they made such things themselves or because their factory had received payment for debt in kind.

Another element of economic reform was the privatization of Russian industries. Reformists in the Yeltsin government sought to speed privatization, believing that only by privatizing factories and enterprises and letting them fight for survival would the economy have any hope of recovering. By the end of 1992, some one-third of enterprises in the services and trade fields had been privatized. The second wave of privatization occurred in 1994–95. However, the process seemed to benefit solely the friends of those in power, who received large chunks of Russian industry for little. In particular, companies in the natural resource sector were sold at prices well below those recommended by the IMF to figures who were close to "the Family," meaning Yeltsin, his daughter, and their allies in the government. From this process emerged the "oligarchs," individuals who, because of their political con-

PROBLEMS WITH THE RUBLE

In 1995 the government, through loans secured from the International Monetary Fund (IMF) and through income from the sale of oil and natural gas, succeeded in stabilizing the national currency by establishing a ruble corridor. This corridor fixed the exchange rate of the ruble that the Russian Central Bank would defend. The rate of inflation dropped, and some stabilization ensued. However, the government continued to borrow large sums of money while avoiding real structural reforms of the economy. By failing to establish an effective tax code and collection mechanisms, clear property rights, and a coherent bankruptcy law and by continued support of failing industries, the government found it increasingly expensive to maintain an artificially set ruble exchange rate. The problem was that the government-set exchange rate did not reflect the country's economic reality and thereby made the ruble the target of speculators. As a result, the ruble collapsed in 1998, and the government was forced to withhold payments on its debt amid a growing number of bankruptcies. The ruble eventually stabilized and inflation diminished, but the living standards of most Russians improved little, though a small proportion of the population became very wealthy. Most economic gains occurred in Moscow, St. Petersburg, and other major urban areas, while vast tracts of Russia faced economic depression.

nections, came to control huge segments of the Russian economy. Many oligarchs bought factories for almost nothing, stripped them, sold what they could, and then closed them, creating huge job losses. By the time Yeltsin left office in 1999, most of the Russian economy had been privatized. The stripping of factories played a major role in the public's disenchantment with the development of capitalism in Russia. The majority of the population saw its living standards drop, social services collapse, and a great rise in crime and corruption.

POLITICAL AND SOCIAL CHANGES

Although Yeltsin had come to represent for many the face of political and economic reform, his first priority was the preservation of his own power and authority. His divide-and-rule strategy led to the emergence of various factions in both the government and the bureaucracy. Indeed, some bureaucrats spent more time in conflict with each other than governing the country. Yeltsin frequently removed ministers and prime ministers, which led to abrupt changes in policy. Throughout his presidency he refused to establish his own political party or to align himself with any party. He believed that the president should remain above party politics, though he was at the heart of the political process, playing the role of power broker—a position he coveted—until his resignation in 1999.

When the Soviet Union collapsed, the Russian Federation continued to be governed according to its Soviet-era constitution, which did not specify which branch—legislative or executive—held supreme power. Political differences manifested themselves as constitutional conflicts.

The government's focus on financial stabilization and economic reform to the apparent neglect of the public's social needs contributed to the growing political battle between the legislative and executive branches. Complicating Yeltsin's difficulties was the fact that many deputies in the parliament had vested interests in the old economic and political structure. The leader of the parliament, Ruslan Khasbulatov, and Yeltsin both sought support from regional elites by promising subsidies and greater local control. The political battle between Yeltsin and Khasbulatov climaxed in March 1993 when Yeltsin was stripped of the decree-making powers that he had been granted after the 1991 coup attempt. Yeltsin was not prepared to accept total defeat. On March 20 Yeltsin announced that he was instituting a presidential regime until April 25, when a referendum would be held over who "really ruled" Russia. He stated that during this period any acts of parliament that contradicted presidential decrees would be null and void. After intense political haggling, Yeltsin was forced to back down. Nonetheless, it was agreed that a referendum would be held on April 25. When the results of the referendum came in, they were a victory for Yeltsin.

That summer Yeltsin established a Constitutional Convention to draw up a new constitution. The parliament also set up its own Constitutional Committee. Inevitably, the drafts were contradictory, and the increasing number of regional leaders who supported the parliamentary version worried Yeltsin. The conflict between

Yeltsin and the parliament continued, growing yet more intense on September 21, 1993, when Yeltsin issued a series of presidential decrees that dissolved the parliament and imposed presidential rule until new parliamentary elections and a referendum on a new draft constitution were held in December. The parliament declared Yeltsin's decree illegal, impeached him, and swore in his vice pres-

1993 offered dramatic scenes of confrontation between Yeltsin and the conservative parliament. These anti-Yeltsin protesters built barricades in central Moscow's Smolenskaya Square on October 2.

ident, Aleksandr Rutskoy, as president. Weapons were handed out to civilians to defend the parliamentary building. On September 25, troops and militia loyal to Yeltsin surrounded the building. On October 2, there were armed clashes between troops and supporters of the Congress. The most serious battle took place around the television station at Ostankino. It seemed a civil war was going to

erupt, prompting Yeltsin to declare a state of emergency in Moscow on October 4. Shortly thereafter, tanks begin firing on the parliamentary building and on the deputies inside, leading to the surrender and arrest of everyone inside the building, including the speaker of the parliament and Rutskoy.

Yeltsin's new constitution gave the president vast powers. The president's decrees had the force of law as long as they did not contradict federal or constitutional law. The prime minister was now appointed by the president (though that appointment would still have to be approved by the

Duma). The president also had the power to dismiss the Duma and call for new parliamentary elections. Although the prime minister was accountable to the parliament, he had to maintain the president's confidence to remain in office. The premiership of Viktor Chernomyrdin (1992–98) reflected the extent to which a Russian prime minister was dependent on the president for his mandate to rule. Yeltsin dismissed Chernomyrdin in 1998, ostensibly for failing to implement reforms energetically enough, though there was the suspicion that the prime minister had offended the president's ego.

In the first two Dumas (elected in 1993 and 1995), the Communist Party of the Russian Federation was the largest party, though it was never close to becoming a majority party. Having inherited the infrastructure of the dissolved Communist Party of the Soviet Union, it had the most effective nationwide organization. Other parties found it difficult to project their message outside the major urban areas. Party loyalties were weak; deputies jumped from one party to another in hope of improving their electoral chances.

The relationship between the Duma and Yeltsin was characterized by public shows of anger and opposition; behind the scenes, however, compromises were more often than not hammered out by political foes. Moreover, Yeltsin had no qualms about threatening the Duma with dissolution when it proved recalcitrant to presidential bills. Deputies, fearful of losing their extensive perks of office and of an electorate angry with all politicians, regularly backed down when faced with the implicit threat of dissolution. During Yeltsin's second term, some deputies tried to initiate impeachment proceedings against him, but Yeltsin easily avoided impeachment.

The weakened Russian state failed to fulfill its basic responsibilities. The legal system, suffering from a lack of resources and trained personnel and a legal code geared to the new market economy, was near collapse. Low salaries led to a drain of experienced jurists to the private sector; there was also widespread corruption within law enforcement and the legal system, as judges and police

ORGANIZED CRIME

One consequence of the political and economic changes of the 1990s was the emergence of Russian organized crime. For most of the Yeltsin administration, shoot-outs between rival groups and the assassinations of organized-crime or business figures filled the headlines of Russian newspapers and created greater disgust among Russians over the course of economic reform and democracy. The explosive rise in crime came as a shock to most Russians, who under the Soviet period had very rarely come into contact with such incidents. The assassinations of well-known and well-liked figures, such as human rights advocate Galina Starovoitova, served to underscore the Yeltsin regime's inability to combat crime. By the end of the Yeltsin era, the open warfare between organized-crime groups had diminished not because of effective state action but because of the consolidation of the remaining criminal groups that had emerged victorious from the bloody struggles.

officials resorted to taking bribes to supplement their meagre incomes. The country's health, education, and social services were also under incredible strain. Due to a lack of resources, law-enforcement agencies proved unable to combat the rising crime. The collapse of medical services led to a decline in life expectancy and to concerns over the negative rate of population growth; doctors and nurses were underpaid, and many hospitals did not have enough resources to provide even basic care.

ETHNIC RELATIONS AND RUSSIA'S "NEAR-ABROAD"

During the Yeltsin years, Russia's numerous regions sought greater autonomy. For example, Tatarstan negotiated additional rights and privileges, and the republic of Chechnya declared independence in 1991, before the collapse of the Soviet Union. Chechen nationalism was based on the struggle against Russian imperialism since the early 19th century and the living memory of Stalin's massive deportations of the Chechen population in 1944 that had resulted in the deaths of a large segment of the population. In late 1994 Yeltsin sent the army into Chechnya after a botched Russian-orchestrated coup against the secessionist president, Dzhokhar Dudayev. There were fears that if Chechnya succeeded in breaking away from the Russian Federation, other republics might follow suit. Moreover, Dudayev's Chechnya had become a source of drug dealing and arms peddling. In 1995 Russia gained control of the capital, Grozny. However, in 1996

Russian forces were pushed out of the capital city. Yeltsin, faced with an upcoming presidential election, had General Aleksandr Lebed sign a cease-fire agreement with the Chechens. The Russians withdrew, postponing the question of Chechen independence.

Moscow coined the term "the near-abroad" when discussing its foreign policy toward the states. Russia hoped to maintain influence over them, and it considered both the Caucasus and Central Asia special areas of interest. Aid from the Russian government to Russian separatists in the Dniester region of Moldova and intervention in the Tajik civil war were illustrative of Moscow's attempt to maintain influence in these areas. In addition, the Russian

These Russian soldiers entered the Chechen stronghold of Bamut in May 1996. By that point, Russian forces had been in Chechnya for over a year, and support for the war there was weakening.

government was prepared to use other means of exerting influence, such as economic pressure on Ukraine and the threat of separatism in Georgia, to attain its ends.

The collapse of the Soviet Union left some 30 million Russians outside the borders of the Russian Federation. The largest Russian populations were in Kazakhstan, Ukraine, and the Baltic countries. Governments in these countries feared that Moscow could, if it wanted, use the Russian populations there to pressure the governments to adopt policies friendly to Moscow. However, Moscow refrained from following such an approach during the 1990s —sometimes to the great criticism of the Russians living in these areas.

FOREIGN AFFAIRS

Yeltsin placed a high priority on relations with the West, particularly the United States. The initial honeymoon period in U.S.-Russian relations ended abruptly, as it became increasingly clear that the countries had different geopolitical goals. One issue was Russia's opposition to the eastward expansion of the North Atlantic Treaty Organization (NATO). Policy disagreements over the Balkans—in particular, U.S. support for armed intervention against the Yugoslav government of Slobodan Milošević—also contributed to the cooling of relations between Washington and Moscow.

The collapse of the Soviet Union left the United States as the sole superpower. Concern with U.S. hegemony in the world system became a constant theme in Russian foreign policy, especially after Yevgeny Primakov became foreign minister in 1995. Primakov stressed the need for a multipolar system of international relations to replace the unipolar world dominated by the United States. In an attempt to counter U.S. power, Moscow strengthened its political and military relations with China and India, although friction between New Delhi and Beijing made a strong trilateral alliance unlikely. Russia's relations with Iran and differences in approaches to Iraq further increased tensions in Russian-U.S. relations.

THE PUTIN PRESIDENCY

Toward the end of Yeltsin's tenure as president, Vladimir Putin began playing a more important role. During the Soviet period, he joined the KGB and worked in East Germany for many years. In July 1998 Putin became director of the Federal Security Service, one of the successor organizations of the KGB, and in August 1999 Yeltsin plucked Putin from relative obscurity for the post of prime minister.

SEPARATISM

As prime minister, Putin blamed Chechen secessionists for the bombing of several apartment buildings that killed scores of Russian civilians, prompting the government to send Russian forces into the republic once again. (Evidence never proved Chechen involvement in these bombings, leading some to believe that the Russian intelligence services played a role.) The campaign enjoyed some initial success, with Grozny falling quickly to the

Many Russians believed that Putin's coolness and decisiveness would help him establish economic and political order in the country and deal with the Chechen problem.

Russians. Putin's popularity soared, and Yeltsin, having chosen Putin as his successor, resigned on December 31, 1999. Putin's first official act as president was to grant Yeltsin a pardon for any illegal activities he might have committed during his administration.

Putin easily defeated Communist Party leader Gennady Zyuganov in the first round of balloting of the March 2000 presidential election. Although the Russian military won control of Chechnya, Chechen fighters fled to the mountains and hills, threatening Russian forces with a prolonged guerilla war. Fighting continued during the next two years, but by 2002 it had abated. Putin, confident in Russia's military position, sought talks with what remained of the Chechen leadership. Nevertheless, in October 2002, Chechen separatists seized a Moscow theatre and threatened to kill all those inside. Putin responded by ordering special forces to raid the theatre, and during the operation some 130 hostages died.

Putin soon reasserted central control over the country's 89 regions by dividing Russia into seven administrative districts, each overseen by a presidential appointee. The new districts were created to root out corruption, keep an eye on the local governors, and ensure that Moscow's will and laws were enforced. During the Yeltsin years, contradictions between Russian federal law and regional law had created chaos in the Russian legal system. Putin worked to establish the supremacy of Russian Federation law throughout the country.

FOREIGN AFFAIRS

Although Putin hoped to maintain a strategic partnership with the United States, he focused on strengthening Russia's relations with Europe. Nevertheless, after the September 11 attacks in 2001 on the United States by al-Qaeda, Putin was the first foreign leader to telephone U.S. President George W. Bush to offer sympathy and help in combating terrorism. Moreover, Russia established a council with NATO on which it sat as an equal alongside NATO's 19 members. Russia also reacted calmly when the United States officially abandoned the Anti-Ballistic Missile Treaty in 2002, established temporary military bases in several former Soviet states in Central Asia, and dispatched special forces on a training mission to Georgia, where there were suspected al-Qaeda training bases. However, Putin was wary of U.S. unilateralism and worked to strengthen Russian ties with China and India and maintain ties with Iran. In 2002–03 he opposed military intervention against Iraq by the United States and the United Kingdom.

Putin strengthened Russia's ties with the Central Asian republics in order to maintain Russian influence. Under Yeltsin the Russian army, starved of funds, had lost much of its effectiveness and technological edge. Russian defeats in the first Chechen war only underlined the appalling state in which the armed forces found itself. Through greater arms sales, Putin hoped to increase funding for the armed forces, particularly for personnel and for the research and development sector of the Russian military industrial complex.

POLITICAL AND ECONOMIC REFORMS

Putin also took steps to limit the political and economic power of the infamous oligarchs. Although Putin could not destroy the business elite, he made it clear that certain limits on their behaviour would be expected. Oligarchs who opposed Putin during the presidential campaign or were critical of his policies faced the Kremlin's wrath. For example, in 2001 Vladimir Gusinsky and Boris Berezovsky, two of Russia's richest men, were stripped of their electronic media holdings. In 2003 Mikhail Khodorkovsky, the former head of the oil giant Yukos, was arrested and eventually convicted of fraud and tax evasion. The campaign against certain oligarchs caused fear among many about Putin's commitment to freedom of speech and the press. Television networks (or their owners) seen as unfriendly to Putin and his policies faced closure by the government—usually on charges of nonpayment of taxes and financial mismanagement.

Although Mikhail Khodorkovsky had been vilified by Putin as an embodiment of the worst excesses of the era of the oligarchs, his imprisonment made him a symbol for proponents of democratic reform in Russia.

Yeltsin's automatic hostility to the Communist Party had resulted in a shaky relationship with the Duma. Putin worked better with it and secured the passage of bills that reformed the tax, judicial, labour, and bankruptcy systems, provided property rights, adopted national symbols and the flag, and approved arms treaties. Unlike Yeltsin, Putin was not inclined to frequent changes in the cabinet or premiership, resulting in policy consistency and political stability that ordinary Russians appreciated.

Despite some opposition, Putin pursued economic reforms. These included a new tax code that simplified the system in order to encourage individuals and businesses to pay taxes and improve the efficiency of collecting taxes. As a result, the state's rate of tax collection dramatically increased. Coupled with a surge in income from the increase in world oil prices, the Russian government enjoyed a budget surplus and was able pay off some of its external debt. Putin was also keen to attract foreign investment in order to reduce Russia's dependence on Western loans (which he believed threatened the country's national interests) and to help finance the refurbishment and expansion of Russian industry. Russia sought to increase its exports by promoting the sale of oil, natural gas, and arms.

Despite criticism that he had centralized too much power in the presidency and was curtailing freedoms, Putin remained popular and was reelected in 2004 in a landslide. During his second term, speculation loomed that he might engineer a change to the constitution to allow him to be reelected yet again. Instead, Putin surprised observers in October 2007 by announcing that he would head the list of the pro-Putin United Russia party in parliamentary elections. In December 2007 United Russia won more than three-fifths of the vote and 315 of the Duma's 450 seats. Putin anointed First Deputy Prime Minister Dmitry Medvedev as his successor. In turn, Medvedev announced that he would appoint Putin prime minister if his campaign succeeded, enabling Putin to continue his dominance of Russian politics. In March 2008, Medvedev was elected president in a contest that some Western election observers considered not fully fair or democratic. Medvedev took office on May 7, 2008, and

Putin was confirmed as Russia's prime minister the following day.

THE MEDVEDEV PRESIDENCY

Three months into his presidency, Medvedev was confronted with a growing military conflict between Russia's neighbour Georgia and South Ossetia, a separatist region of Georgia that borders the Russian republic of North Ossetia–Alania. As fighting between Georgian and Ossetian forces escalated in August 2008, Russia sent troops across the border with the goal of supporting rebels in not only South Ossetia but also Abkhazia, another separatist region within Georgia. In response to condemnation from NATO, Russia suspended its cooperation with the Atlantic alliance. In September the Russian government agreed to withdraw its troops from Georgia. However, it planned to maintain a military presence in South Ossetia and Abkhazia, whose independence it had recognized.

The central message of Medvedev's presidential campaign was "Freedom is better than no freedom," a remark that hinted at an openness to the West that was uncharacteristic of the Putin years.

Meanwhile, sporadic fighting between Russian forces and local militants continued elsewhere in the Caucasus region, particularly in the Russian republics of Ingushetiya and Chechnya. By early 2009 the conflict in Chechnya appeared to have abated. That April Medvedev announced the end of Russia's counterinsurgency operations there. Despite this official pronouncement, clashes between security forces and militants in the Caucasus continued, as did militant attacks on local officials and infrastructure. In March 2010 suicide bombers, believed to be linked to an extremist group in the Caucasus, detonated explosives that killed more than three dozen people in the Moscow Metro.

As 2011 progressed, Russians wondered if Medvedev would stand for reelection. He ended months of speculation in September 2011 when he announced that he and Putin would, in essence, trade jobs. Putin would run for president and, if elected, would likely appoint Medvedev prime minister. The plan for a seamless succession hit a snag on December 4, 2011, when United Russia lost the two-thirds majority that allowed it to make changes to the constitution. International observers characterized the election as lacking fairness. Within days of the election, an estimated 50,000 people gathered near the Kremlin to protest the results. Putin dismissed them and claimed that the protesters were "paid agents of the West." Independent analyses of the December vote uncovered irregularities, including statistically unlikely voter turnout levels and final results that were wildly at odds with preliminary counts. Organized protests continued into 2012, and in February of that year an estimated 30,000 people formed a human chain around the centre of Moscow.

THE SECOND PUTIN PRESIDENCY

On March 4, 2012, Putin was elected to a third term as president of Russia. His first year back in office was characterized by a largely successful effort to stifle the protest movement. Opposition leaders were jailed, and nongovernmental organizations that received funding from abroad were labeled "foreign agents." Tensions with the United States flared in June 2013, when U.S. National Security Agency (NSA) contractor Edward Snowden found refuge in Russia after revealing the existence of a number of secret NSA programs. After chemical weapons attacks outside Damascus in August 2013, the U.S. made the case for military intervention in the Syrian Civil War. In an editorial published in the *New York Times*, Putin urged restraint, and U.S. and Russian officials brokered a deal whereby Syria's chemical weapons supply would be destroyed.

THE UKRAINE CONFLICT AND SYRIAN INTERVENTION

In February 2014, the government of Ukrainian President Viktor Yanukovych was overthrown after months of pro-test. Yanukovych fled to Russia. Refusing to recognize the interim government in Kiev as legitimate, Putin requested parliamentary approval to dispatch troops to Ukraine. By early March 2014 Russian troops and pro-Russian paramilitary groups had effectively taken control of the Crimea. In a popular referendum held on March 16, residents of the Crimea voted to join Russia. In protest, Western governments introduced a series of travel bans and asset freezes against members of Putin's inner circle. On March 21 Putin signed legislation that formalized the Russian annexation of Crimea.

In April 2014, groups of unidentified gunmen outfitted with Russian equipment seized government buildings throughout southeastern Ukraine, sparking an armed conflict with the government in Kiev. Putin referred to the region as Novorossiya ("New Russia"), evoking claims from the imperial era. Although all signs pointed to direct Russian involvement in the insurgency, Putin steadfastly denied having a hand in the fighting. On July 17, 2014, Malaysia Airlines flight MH17 crashed in eastern Ukraine, and overwhelming evidence indicated that it had been shot down by a Russian-made surface-to-air missile fired from rebel-controlled territory. Western countries responded by tightening sanctions. This, combined with plummeting oil prices, sent the Russian economy into a tailspin. NATO estimated that more than 1,000 Russian troops were actively fighting inside Ukraine when Russian and Ukrainian leaders met for cease-fire talks in Minsk, Belarus, on September 5. The cease-fire slowed, but did not stop, the violence, and pro-Russian rebels spent the following months pushing back Ukrainian government forces.

In February 2014, armed militants took control of government buildings in Simferopol, the capital of the Crimea. They wore uniforms without insignia but were believed to have connections to the Russian military.

On February 12, 2015, Putin met with world leaders to approve a peace plan aimed at ending the fighting in Ukraine. Although fighting slowed for a period, the conflict picked up again in the spring. By September 2015 the UN estimated that some 8,000 people had been killed and 1.5 million had been displaced. On September 28, 2015, in an address before the UN General Assembly, Putin presented his vision of Russia as a world power, capable of projecting its influence abroad, while painting the United States and NATO as threats to global security. Two days later Russia became an active participant in the Syrian Civil War, when Russian aircraft struck targets near the cities of Homs and Hama. Although Russian defense officials stated that the air strikes were intended to target troops and matériel belonging to the Islamic State in Iraq and the Levant, the actual focus of the attacks seemed to have been opponents of Syrian president and Russian ally Bashar al-Assad.

SILENCING CRITICS AND ACTIONS IN THE WEST

On February 27, 2015, opposition leader Boris Nemtsov was gunned down just days after he speaking out against Russian intervention in Ukraine. Nemtsov was only the latest Putin critic to die under suspicious circumstances. In January 2016 a British public inquiry officially implicated Putin in the 2006 murder of former Federal Security Service (FSB; the successor to the KGB) officer Alexander Litvinenko, who had spoken out against Russian government ties to organized crime. Litvinenko was poisoned with polonium-210 while drinking tea in a London hotel.

Aleksey Navalny, an opposition activist who achieved prominence as a leader of the 2011 protest movement, was repeatedly imprisoned on what supporters characterized as politically motivated charges. Navalny finished second in the Moscow mayoral race in 2013, but his Progress Party was shut out of subsequent elections on procedural grounds. In the September 2016 legislative election, voter turnout was just 47.8 percent, the lowest since the collapse of the Soviet Union. Voter apathy was attributed to Putin's steady implementation of so-called "managed democracy," a system whereby the basic struc-

ПУТИН— ПОСЛЕДНЕЕ ПРИБЕЖИЩЕ НЕГОДЯЕВ!

This protest in memory of Boris Nemtsov took place on March 1, 2015. Nemtsov was a physicist, politician, and outspoken critic of Putin.

tures and procedures of democracy were maintained but the outcome of elections was largely predetermined. Putin's United Russia party claimed victory, but election observers documented numerous irregularities. Navalny's party was prohibited from fielding any candidates, and Nemtsov's PARNAS received less than 1 percent of the vote.

By 2016 evidence emerged that Russia was conducting a wide-ranging campaign intended to undermine the legitimacy of Western democracies. Many of the attacks blurred the line between cyberwarfare and cybercrime, while others recalled the direct Soviet interventionism of the Cold War era. Russian fighter jets routinely violated NATO airspace in the Baltic, and a pair of sophisticated cyberattacks on the Ukrainian power grid plunged hundreds of thousands of people into darkness. Ukrainian President Petro Poroshenko reported that his country had been subjected to more than 6,000 cyber intrusions over a two-month period, with virtually every sector of Ukrainian society being targeted. Poroshenko stated that Ukrainian investigators had linked the cyberwar campaign to Russian security services. In Montenegro, where the pro-Western government was preparing for accession to NATO, authorities narrowly averted a plot to assassinate Prime Minister Milo Đjukanović and install a pro-Russian government. Montenegrin prosecutors uncovered a conspiracy that linked nationalist Serbs, pro-Russian fighters in eastern Ukraine, and, allegedly, a pair of Russian intelligence agents who had orchestrated the planned coup.

In the months prior to the 2016 U.S. presidential election, a series of hacking attacks targeted the Democratic Party and its presidential nominee Hillary Clinton. Computer security experts tied these attacks to Russian intelligence services, and in July 2016 thousands of private e-mails were published by WikiLeaks. Within days the FBI opened a probe into Russian efforts to influence the presidential election. It was later revealed that this investigation was also examining possible connections between those efforts and the campaign of Republican presidential candidate Donald Trump. Trump joked that Russia had released the hacked e-mails because "Putin likes me" and later invited Russia to "find [Clinton's] 30,000 e-mails that are missing." In spite of these statements,

Trump repeatedly dismissed the possibility that Putin was attempting to sway the election in his favour.

After Trump's victory in November 2016, renewed attention was focused on the cyberattacks and possible collusion between Trump's campaign team and Russia. U.S. intelligence agencies concluded that Putin had ordered a multipronged campaign to influence the election and undermine faith in American democratic systems. U.S. President Barack Obama imposed economic sanctions on Russian intelligence services and expelled dozens of suspected Russian operatives, but Trump continued to reject the conclusions of U.S. intelligence agencies.

For his part, Putin denied the existence of any campaign to influence foreign elections. In May 2017, another cyberattack was attributed to Fancy Bear, the Russian government-linked group that had carried out the hack on the Democratic Party. France was holding the second round of its presidential election, and the finalists were centrist Emmanuel Macron and far-right National Front candidate Marine Le Pen. Le Pen had previously received financial support from a bank with ties to the Kremlin, and she vowed to push for the end of the sanctions that had been enacted after Russia's annexation of Crimea. Just hours before a media blackout on campaign-related news coverage went into effect, a massive trove of internal communications dubbed "MacronLeaks" surfaced on the Internet. This effort came to naught, as Macron captured nearly twice as many votes as Le Pen.

His inability to rally popular support with sustained economic prosperity was what forced Putin to appeal to patriotic fervor and to highlight Russia's differences with the West. The shift in focus was gradual, but definitively took hold by 2012. In the intervening years, Putin has been committed to reestablishing Russia as a great power. That shift has proven considerably risky, however, not only for Russia but also for the rest of the international community.

Putin's foreign moves appeared to produce significant dividends at home, as his popular approval rating consistently remained above 80 percent despite Russia's sluggish economy and endemic government corruption. Low oil prices and Western sanctions compounded an already grim financial outlook as foreign investors remained reluctant to put their capital at risk in a land where personal ties to Putin were seen as more important than the rule of law. Even after Russia emerged from seven consecutive quarters of recession, wages and consumer spending remained stagnant in 2017. These and other domestic problems seemed to do little to dent Putin's image, though; among those expressing concern for such issues in opinion polls, blame was most often affixed to Putin's prime minister, Dmitry Medvedev.

ANARCHISM A cluster of doctrines and attitudes centred on the belief that government is both harmful and unnecessary.

ANNEX To incorporate (a territory) within one's own domain.

ARABLE Suitable for the growing of crops.

AUTOCRACY A government in which one person has unlimited power.

AUTONOMOUS Having the right to self-govern, at least to some degree.

BOURGEOIS Referring to a person whose social behavior and political views are held to be influenced by interest in private property.

CAPITALISM The economic system, dominant in the Western world since the breakup of feudalism, in which most of the means of production are privately owned and production is guided and income distributed largely through the operation of markets.

COMMUNISM The political and economic doctrine that aims to replace private property and a profit-based economy with public ownership and communal control of at least the major means of production (such as mines, mills, and factories) and the natural resources of a society.

CONCESSION Something granted, often grudgingly.

COUNTERINSURGENCY Organized military activity designed to combat an uprising.

DEPORTATION The removal from a country of a person (often a non-citizen) whose presence is determined to be unlawful or harmful to the public.

DÉTENTE A relaxation of strained relations or tensions (as between nations).

EXPROPRIATION The taking away of property or the right to property.

GENDARME A member of an armed national police force.

GROSS DOMESTIC PRODUCT (GDP) The total value of the goods and services produced in a country during a specific period of time, usually a year.

GYMNASIUM A state-maintained secondary school, particularly in Germany, that prepares pupils for higher academic education.

HEGEMONY The social, cultural, ideological, or economic influence exerted by a dominant group.

INFLATION Collective increases in the supply of money, in money incomes, or in prices. Inflation is generally thought of as an inordinate rise in the general level of prices.

INTERVENTIONISM The interference by one country in the political affairs of another.

MATÉRIEL Equipment, apparatus, and supplies used by an organization or institution.

OLIGARCHY Government by the few, especially despotic power exercised by a small and privileged group for corrupt or selfish purposes.

OPERATIVE A person who works toward achieving the objectives of a larger interest, sometimes as a secret agent.

PRIVATIZATION The transfer of government services or assets to the private sector.

PROLETARIAN Relating to the class of wage workers who were engaged in industrial production and whose chief source of income was derived from the sale of their labour power.

PROPAGANDA The dissemination of information—facts, arguments, rumours, half-truths, or lies—to influence public opinion.

SERF A tenant farmer who was bound to a hereditary plot of land and to the will of his landlord.

SOCIALISM The social and economic doctrine that calls for public rather than private ownership or control of property and natural resources.

ZEMSTVO An organ of rural self-government in the Russian Empire and Ukraine; established in 1864 to provide social and economic services, it became a significant liberal influence within imperial Russia.

BIBLIOGRAPHY

General surveys of Russian history in the 19th century include David Saunders, *Russia in the Age of Reaction and Reform, 1801–1881* (1992); and Hugh Seton-Watson, *The Russian Empire, 1801–1917* (1967, reprinted 1990). An excellent English-language work on the reign of Alexander I is Janet M. Hartley, *Alexander I* (1994). Politics during the reign of Alexander I is discussed in Alexander M. Martin, *Romantics, Reformers, and Reactionaries: Russian Conservative Thought and Politics in the Reign of Alexander I* (1997). The reign of Nicholas I is explored in W. Bruce Lincoln, *Nicholas I, Emperor and Autocrat of All the Russias* (1978, reprinted 1989). The general economic development of Russia in the 19th century is analyzed in W. Bruce Lincoln, *The Great Reforms: Autocracy, Bureaucracy, and the Politics of Change in Imperial Russia* (1990); Ben Eklof, John Bushnell, and Larissa Zakharova (eds.), *Russia's Great Reforms, 1855–1881* (1994); and Arcadius Kahan, *Russian Economic History: The Nineteenth Century*, ed. by Roger Weiss (1989). An analysis of reform and counterreform dynamics is given in Thomas S. Pearson, *Russian Officialdom in Crisis: Autocracy and Local Self-Government, 1861–1900* (1989, reissued 2002). Dominic Lieven, *Nicholas II* (1993, reissued 1996), examines the personality of Nicholas II and his reign.

Studies of important issues in Russian foreign policy and the emergence of the Russian Empire include William C. Fuller, Jr., *Strategy and Power in Russia, 1600–1914* (1992); Dietrich Geyer, *Russian Imperialism: The Interaction of Domestic and Foreign Policy, 1860–1914*, trans. by

Bruce Little (1987; originally published in German, 1977); Andreas Kappeler, *The Russian Empire: A Multiethnic History*, trans. by Alfred Clayton (2001; originally published in German, 1992); Dominic Lieven, *Empire: The Russian Empire and Its Rivals* (2000, reissued 2003); and Geoffrey Hosking, *Russia: People and Empire, 1552–1917* (1997).

An excellent general introduction to the period is Hans Rogger, *Russia in the Age of Modernisation and Revolution, 1881–1917* (1983). Foreign policy is the subject of Barbara Jelavich, *Russia's Balkan Entanglements, 1806–1914* (1991, reissued 2002); David MacLaren McDonald, *United Government and Foreign Policy in Russia, 1900–1914* (1992); and Dominic Lieven, *Russia and the Origins of the First World War* (1983). Dominic Lieven, *Russia's Rulers Under the Old Regime* (1989), offers a collective portrait of the policy makers. The economy of the period is examined in Peter Gatrell, *The Tsarist Economy, 1850–1917* (1986).

The Revolution of 1905 is addressed in Abraham Ascher, *The Revolution of 1905*, 2 vol. (1988–92); and Andrew M. Verner, *The Crisis of Russian Autocracy: Nicholas II and the 1905 Revolution* (1990). A more comparative socio-economic approach to the revolution is demonstrated in Teodor Shanin, *The Roots of Otherness: Russia's Turn of Century*, 2 vol. (1986), which concentrates especially on the peasantry. The reaction of the elites to the revolution is analyzed in Roberta Thompson Manning, *The Crisis of the Old Order in Russia: Gentry and Government* (1982). The politics of the new parliament, the Duma, is outlined in Geoffrey A. Hosking, *The Russian Constitutional Experiment:*

Government and Duma, 1907–1914 (1973); and the social dimension of the new politics is examined in Leopold H. Haimson (ed.), *The Politics of Rural Russia, 1905–1914* (1979); and Victoria E. Bonnell, *Roots of Rebellion: Workers' Politics and Organizations in St. Petersburg and Moscow, 1900–1914* (1983). Russia's problems during World War I are described in Michael T. Florinsky, *The End of the Russian Empire* (1931, reprinted 1973). The revolutionary period is the subject of Orlando Figes, *A People's Tragedy* (1996, reissued 1998).

For the Soviet period there are few specific histories of Russia, which is always treated in the wider context of the Soviet Union. An overview of the Revolution of 1917 and its consequences is offered in Sheila Fitzpatrick, *The Russian Revolution*, 2nd ed. (1994, reissued 2001). Robert Service, *A History of Twentieth-Century Russia* (1998), is a history of the Soviet state. Christopher Read, *The Making and Breaking of the Soviet System* (2001), analyzes the causes of the rise and fall of the Soviet Union. Relevant historical biographies include Robert Service, *Lenin: A Biography* (2000); Robert C. Tucker, *Stalin as Revolutionary, 1879–1929* (1973), and *Stalin in Power, 1928–1941* (1990); and William J. Tompson, *Khrushchev: A Political Life* (1995, reissued 1997). Chris Ward (ed.), *The Stalinist Dictatorship* (1998), is a readable examination of the Stalinist period. The Gorbachev era is analyzed in Archie Brown, *The Gorbachev Factor* (1996); Stephen White, *After Gorbachev*, 4th ed. (1994), a solid narrative of the years of perestroika; Richard Sakwa, *Gorbachev and His Reforms, 1985–1990* (1990); Jeffrey F. Hough, *Democratization and Revolution* in the USSR, 1985–1991 (1997); and *Mikhail Gorbachev, Perestroika: New Thinking for Our Country and the World*, new, updated ed. (1988), and *Memoirs* (1996), which reveals insights into Gorbachev's thinking. Good introductions to the Soviet political structure and situation are Richard Sakwa, *Soviet Politics in Perspective*, 2nd ed. rev. (1998); Gordon B. Smith, *Soviet Politics: Struggling with Change*, 2nd ed. (1992); Geoffrey Ponton, *The Soviet Era: Soviet Politics from Lenin to Yeltsin* (1994); and Evan Mawdsley and Stephen White, *The Soviet Elite from Lenin to Gorbachev: The Central Committee and Its Members, 1917–1991* (2000), a wide-ranging survey. Alec Nove, *An Economic History of the USSR, 1917–1991*, 3rd ed. (1992), is an informed, accessible account. The breakup of the Soviet Union is the subject of Ronald Grigor Suny, *The Revenge of the Past: Nationalism, Revolution, and the Collapse of the Soviet Union* (1993); and Roman Szporluk, *Russia, Ukraine, and the Break-up of the Soviet Union* (2000). Foreign policy is discussed in Gabriel Gorodetsky (ed.), *Soviet Foreign Policy, 1917–1991: A Retrospective* (1994). Vladislav Zubok and Constantine Pleshakov, *Inside the Kremlin's Cold War: From Stalin to Khrushchev* (1996), uses archival material released in the 1990s to examine the Cold War and its origins from the Soviet point of view. The secret police's role during the Soviet period is the subject of Amy W. Knight, *The KGB: Police and Politics in the Soviet Union*, rev. ed. (1990).

Interpretative surveys include Lilia Shevtsova, *Yeltsin's Russia: Myth and Reality* (2000); Stephen White, Alex Pravda, and Zvi Gitelman (eds.), *Developments in Rus-*

sian Politics 5, 5th ed. (2001); and Archie Brown (ed.), *Contemporary Russian Politics: A Reader* (2001). Studies of the economic transition include Andrei Shleifer and Daniel Treisman, *Without a Map: Political Tactics and Economic Reform in Russia* (2000); Alena V. Ledeneva, *Russia's Economy of Favours: Blat, Networking, and Informal Exchange* (1998); Jefferey F. Hough, *The Logic of Economic Reform in Russia* (2001); Thane Gustafson, *Capitalism Russian-Style* (1999); Peter Reddaway and Dmitri Glinski, *The Tragedy of Russia's Reforms: Market Bolshevism Against Democracy* (2001); and Tim McDaniel, *The Agony of the Russian Idea* (1996). Geoffrey Hosking and Robert Service (eds.), *Russian Nationalism, Past and Present* (1997), examines the reemergence of Russian identity since the collapse of the U.S.S.R. The conflict in Chechnya is explored in John B. Dunlop, *Russia Confronts Chechnya: Roots of a Separatist Conflict* (1998); and Anatol Lieven, *Chechnya: Tombstone of Russian Power* (1998). A solid account of Russian foreign policy in the Yeltsin years is Ted Hopf (ed.), *Understandings of Russian Foreign Policy* (1999).

Leon Aron, *Yeltsin: A Revolutionary Life* (2000), is an excellent biography. The institutional and political context in which Russian democracy emerged in the 1990s is the subject of Graeme Gill and Roger D. Markwick, *Russia's Stillborn Democracy?: From Gorbachev to Yeltsin* (2000); Gordon B. Smith (ed.), *State-Building in Russia: The Yeltsin Legacy and the Challenge of the Future* (1999); and Valerie Sperling (ed.), *Building the Russian State: Institutional Crisis and the Quest for Democratic Governance* (2000).